Praise for *The ACoA Trauma Syndrome*

"For people with addiction or mental illness in their family of origin, this book is an excellent place to start. It integrates scientific research with practical recovery knowledge, offering the reader a complete picture."

—**Patrick J. Carnes, PhD,** author of the national bestseller *Out of the Shadows*

"Once again, Tian Dayton has shown us that she has the clearest path to recovery for survivors of trauma."

—**Phil Diaz**, coauthor of *Healing Trauma Through Self-Parenting* and founding board member of NACoA

"In this remarkable and deeply compassionate book, Dr. Dayton considers addiction in the context of neurobiology, trauma treatment, and attachment research. Demonstrating that human beings are hardwired to seek and maintain attachment, she describes parental addiction is a profound unresolved loss for children of alcoholics. Dr. Dayton points out that this traumatic attachment rupture lives on as "dissociated capsules" that reverberate into adulthood and across generations. This book is a "must read" not only for adult children of alcoholics, to whom she offers hope, healing and practical advice, but also for anyone seeking an understanding of how attachment and trauma research can inform contemporary addiction treatment."

—**Donna Wick, EdD**, Executive Director, Freedom Institute

"Tian Dayton's new book should be required reading for policy and program makers at all levels of government—and reading it will not be a chore. With clarity and insight, her beautiful writing captures both the chronic pain of growing up in a highly stressed, dysfunctional family and the later effects such experiences can have on children whose submerged feelings may resurface and affect their parenting and interpersonal relationships for generations. These are not the headline-catching stories of families torn apart by hurricanes or war, but the far more pervasive and equally wrenching dramas that play out in the living rooms of families impacted by addiction and dysfunction. We incur a high cost in dollars and public health by failing to take a comprehensive approach to the healing of such families. Dayton's important book offers a rare window into the reality of family life for millions of Americans affected by the programs or lack of programs intended to address these issues."

—**Alan Levitt**, former Associate Director of the White House Drug Policy Office and Director of the National Youth Anti-Drug Media Campaign

"Dr. Dayton has done something no one else thought to do: she's conjured, in a mind-altering way, the missing piece of the puzzle to wholeness from the ACoA state of being. Her curiosity for cause and condition is overshadowed only by her ability to story tell in a delicious, engaging way."

—**Brad Lamm**, BR-I, Addiction Expert and
Author of *How to Help the One You Love*

"Dayton does it again! Prepare yourself for a treat: complex, beautifully composed, easily digestible, and satisfying. Tian Dayton paints a nuanced, comprehensive picture of the impact of childhood trauma on the developing brain, the developing child, and the emerging adult, completing this by a comprehensive approach to healing ourselves spiritually, mentally, physically as individuals, partners, and parents. A must read."

—**Patricia O'Gorman, PhD**, coauthor of *Healing Trauma Through Self-Parenting*
and author of *Dancing Backwards in High Heels*

"Tian Dayton's writings have brought me closer to the man my dogs think I am! Every morning I start my day with Tian Dayton. She is the muse to everything that is good in our universe. Reading Tian personally helped me find my smile again."

—**Joey Pantoliano**, Actor (*The Sopranos, The Fugitive*), Filmmaker, Creator of
No Kidding Me Too NKM2!, and *New York Times* Bestselling
Author of *Asylum: Hollywood Tales of My Great Depression*

"Dr. Tian Dayton hits a home run with her new book, *The ACoA Trauma Syndrome*. She clearly, succinctly, and powerfully describes the experience of growing up in an addicted family. Tian brilliantly provides a road map to healing, recovery, and resilience. This is a must read."

—**Jerry Moe, MA**, National Director
of Children's Programs, Betty Ford Center

"Dayton lays out an insightful, compassionate, and expansive view of the lifelong effects of growing up in addicted families. This book is laced with references to science, but more importantly to her own personal experience and the experiences of her clients who are on the journey of recovery, healing, and breaking the intergenerational cycles of addiction."

—**Robert Anda, MD**, ACE Study Concepts

"Tian Dayton's work in *The ACOA Trauma Syndrome* makes sense of the emotional, physical, and psychological pain that can result from growing up in a family affected by substance abuse. She gives readers an understanding of seemingly random physiological or emotional responses to life events that continue to occur throughout adulthood, and she offers valuable insights and tips that will allow readers to start to heal both mind and body.

—**Deni Carise, PhD**, Chief Clinical Officer,
Phoenix House Foundation New York

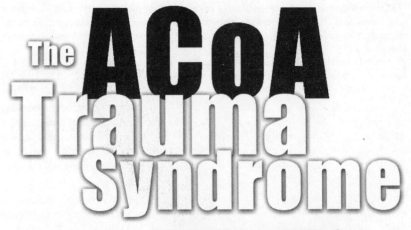

The ACoA Trauma Syndrome

The Impact of **Childhood Pain**
on Adult Relationships

Tian Dayton, PhD

Health Communications, Inc.
Deerfield Beach, Florida

www.hcibooks.com

While examples and case studies presented in this book are real, the names and identifying characteristics of companies and individuals have been altered to protect their confidentiality. As such, any resemblance to a specific individual or company is coincidental.

The ideas and advice contained in this book may not apply to every individual and situation. You should consult with a professional where appropriate. The author shall not be liable for any loss or damage allegedly arising from any information or advice contained in this book.

Library of Congress Cataloging-in-Publication Data
is available throught the Library of Congress

©2012 Tian Dayton

ISBN 13: 978-0-7573-1644-9 (paperback)
ISBN 10: 0-7573-1644-1 (paperback)
ISBN 13: 978-0-7573-1645-6 (e-book)
ISBN 10: 0-7573-1645-X (e-book)

HCI, its logos, and marks are trademarks of Health Communications, Inc.

Publisher: Health Communications, Inc.
        3201 S.W. 15th Street
        Deerfield Beach, FL 33442–8190

Cover design by Dane Wesolko
Interior design by Lawna Patterson Oldfield
Interior formatting by Dawn Von Strolley Grove

Contents

Acknowledgments

This book is lovingly and gratefully dedicated to my husband, Brandt. We have held each other's hands for most of our lives as partners and as parents, and we have walked this path of healing our mutual ACoA legacies together, each of us understanding the deep pain that we carried from being so devoted to a parent who we lost to the disease of addiction.

I know that each of us is responsible for our own happiness and we take that seriously, but my child's heart is happy next to Brandt's, and it is his friendship, motivation, and support in this journey that have made it what it is.

He and I join together in thanking our beautiful children, Marina and Alex, and our wonderful son-in-law, Jasper. They have grown into the kind of adults who are not only a primary source of pride, support, joy, and fun for us, but also our best friends. We could not feel happier or more grateful for their love and presence in our lives. It is they who have motivated us to become better people.

The confidentiality attached to the work that therapists do means that many of the people closest and most vital to their (our) work will always remain nameless. So thank you to my clients and students for the joys, sorrows, tears, and laughter. And thank you for so generously sharing your stories in this book.

Special appreciation to my mom and stepdad, Elaine and Walt Walker, for their courage in facing addiction in an era that hid from it and for pointing the way out to me at such a young age through their life-long support and interest in this area. And heart-felt thanks to both my family and my husband's family (who have all struggled with addiction of parents and grandparents) for being together on this path out. It has meant so much to have such intelligent, caring, and—to a person—hilariously funny company on this journey.

The National Association for Children of Alcoholics is the oldest advocacy organization for children living with family addiction or dysfunction. It is NACoA's mission to educate and elevate awareness, so that CoAs can be helped to come out of emotional hiding and mobilize their own resilience. Learn more at www.nacoa.org.

Many thanks to both my daughter, Marina Dayton, for her elegant and user-friendly design and David George of Ontra Studios, for their tireless and generous help in creating emotion-explorer.com, the interactive self-help website that can be used as a companion to this book.

Thanks to everyone at Health Communications for their support and hard work on this book. Many thanks to my wonderful and perspicacious editor Candace Johnson for her help every step of the way and to Tonya Woodworth for preparing the manuscript. And as always, I extend a special thank you to Peter Vegso and Gary Seidler, heads of Health Communications and U. S. Journal and Training conferences, who have done so much to bring ACoA issues into the public eye. I cannot thank these men enough for their support and friendship throughout my career.

Introduction

The psychological rule says that when an inner situation is not made conscious, it happens outside, as fate. That is to say, when the individual . . . does not become conscious of his inner opposite, the world must perforce act out the conflict and be torn into opposing halves.

—Carl Jung

My father had two very distinct personalities. The same father who tenderly gave me café au lait on a spoon and fresh-squeezed orange juice in a baby glass, who listened to my childish sentences with such pride and pleasure, who dreamed impossible dreams for my future and worked all of his life to give me the best of everything—that same beloved father had a monster living inside of him. And that monster was as frightening to me as the other side of him was beautiful. And that monster grew stronger with each drink he took. At different times of the month, the week, and eventually the day, the monster would take over my father, and I would have no idea where my "real" dad had gone.

Now and then, the monster in him would break loose and

dance with the monster in all of us. The monster roared its terrible roar and sat in my father's chair in the living room. And I was, somehow, this monster's child. We each, at one time or another, shared his private hell with him until all of us lost our grip on normal.

But still, this was *my* family, *my* dad, *my* monster, and I had to do something to make emotional and psychological sense of living with a parent who made me feel both safe and terrified; a parent whom I loved and hated all at once. All children are faced with integrating parts of their parents that they both love and hate, but for the child in the alcoholic home, this becomes a uniquely challenging and daily experience.

When Dad went to (and left) treatment, there was no such thing as family healing. The wisdom of the day was essentially "get the alcoholic sober and the rest of the family will get better automatically." But that didn't happen. It didn't happen because the de-selfing experience of living on an emotional roller coaster had left us not knowing what normal life felt like. The healthy boundary that once surrounded the sweet and secure membrane of our lives was invaded and degraded by the disease of addiction. Just as we had a drunken father and a sober one, we had a drunken family and a sober one. It was as if we repeatedly passed behind some invisible curtain, reemerging each time into an alternate universe but still in our same, familiar living room. The scenes looked somewhat the same, but they felt different. Just maneuvering in and through these worlds required creative, complex, zany, and sometimes rather dysfunctional strategies.

We had no idea, in the 1960s, of how deeply affected an entire

family becomes, how the trauma of living with the daily disruptions, distortions, and denial of addiction wraps its tentacles
around childhood development and family development, changing everyone. But it doesn't have to be that way. Today we have
something called recovery. Today we recognize that there is no
dignity in hiding the truth and no freedom in keeping secrets.
We learn, in recovery, to stand up and take responsibility for the
part of the disease that lives in us and to take the necessary steps
to treat it. And in doing this, we restore our hope, faith, and trust
in life.

It is impossible to explain to someone who has not been
through it how many little things go awry in a home where
addiction has taken hold. Sure, I can say routines were thrown
off; there was constant crisis that wasn't there before, but that
doesn't fully describe it. What really hurts is that you can no longer count on anyone the way that you once did. You watch the
parent you love turn the face that once smiled at you towards a
bottle of alcohol or sink into a lying and degrading behavior. And
then, just as mysteriously, he returns, clean-shaven, loving you
once again, and remembering all the things you worried he had
forgotten--that you're in a school play, what you like for breakfast, that you are still there (even though he comes and goes).
You have him back. You're torn between letting it feel wonderful (which it does) and not letting it feel too good, because you
know from experience that if it feels too good it will only hurt
more when he slips away again. Then sure enough, you sense
tension creeping in, you see situations devolving and unraveling
before your eyes, and you know that it's coming. You can read

all the signs. The gap between the worlds that had temporarily closed up begins to widen, and your addict disappears into some crevice, some wormhole in the universe, and he is gone as mysteriously as he came. He returns to his private nowhere where you can't find him. He hides in plain sight. And you have to lose him once again. And wait to see what happens. And just be in the family that is still there. Somewhat there. You see the disappointment on the faces around you; you see the confusion, the humiliation and the hurt. And simultaneously you see those family members shake their heads, square their shoulders, and mush on because the world is still chugging along even though the alcoholic has stepped off. You both appreciate and hate their efforts. You appreciate the ones who are able to plow through, even with blinders, because someone has to, because there are school buses to make, homework to be done, and appointments to get to. You hate it because you sense the sham underneath it. The pain inside you, inside everyone grows. But no one talks about it; because what would they say? It is too sad to look at, too much to sort out.

And changing one person might mean everyone has to change. And what would that mean--what would it look like and who would everyone be then? And besides, the family loses track of what's wrong. Is it even the alcohol you are looking at? Or the debting? Or the sexual liaisons and secrets? You hardly know any more. Addicts are so good at hiding their disease that for years it simply reads as their personality, their "depression," their "negativity," their "expansive personality."

◊◊◊◊

The Japanese said it most succinctly: "First the man takes the drink, then the drink takes the drink, then the drink takes the man." And I would add that then the drink or disease takes the family. This disease is contagious. It's not only the addict who needs to sober up. Family members, too, need to become emotionally sober. Today, because treatment is so much more common, its progression can be caught before it spreads through the whole family. But the longer a family remains silent, in denial and living in the throes of managing the mind-numbing disease of addiction, the more symptomatic family members are likely to become.

Adult children of alcoholics (ACoAs) can and often do suffer from some features of post-traumatic stress disorder (PTSD) that are the direct result of living with the traumatizing effects of addiction. Years after we leave behind our alcoholic homes, we carry the impact of living with addiction with us. We import past, unresolved pain into present-day relationships, but without much awareness as to how or why. And that is what this book is about. How living with addiction or dysfunction creates cumulative trauma, the effects of which can play out over a life time. And what to do to get better. And how getting better will open doors inside of you that you hardly knew were there.

Family Trauma Need Not Be a Life Sentence

Trauma is actually fairly common; most people grow up with at least four adverse childhood experiences (Anda 2006). It is not necessarily the trauma that creates lasting problematic effects, but how we deal with it (or don't deal with it) when it occurs and afterward. Much can be done to ameliorate the effects of adverse childhood experiences. Supportive people, places to go that feel safe, and moving shock into some form of consciousness so pain does not remain hidden and unspoken can take a situation that could be traumatic and turn it into something that might be less damaging and potentially even character building.

Our culture creates a sort of myth of "happily ever after" that is really no one's life. Feeling sad, anxious, or fearful is part of the human condition and does not necessarily require treatment. What makes trauma different from normal life stressors is that its effects tend to be long-lasting and repetitive and the patterns that are associated with a traumatic circumstance make their way through the generations. Our shock is long-lasting, engraved in our neurological systems and evidenced by how easily we can be triggered, how quickly our emotions go from zero to ten. We experience a loss of neuromodulation, which translates into our losing some of our ability to self regulate. Feelings, even intense ones, come and go; but unresolved, hidden and unprocessed trauma can last.

Because of the way the brain processes trauma, our most painful experiences may be the very ones that get repressed or thrown out of conscious awareness. While initially this allows us to function during overwhelming experiences that might otherwise immobilize us, eventually those feelings of fear and anxiety need to be felt rather than frozen. The family, while a perfect unit for raising young, can also be fertile ground for creating cumulative trauma throughout the developmental cycle.

Our primary relationships are meant to nurture and sustain us until we are strong enough to survive on our own. When small children are terrified by the very same people who they would normally go to for comfort and safety, they become trapped in a confusing and disequilibrating system with no one to help them to restore their sense of "normal" and their feeling of emotional balance. They are then forced to come up with immature strategies to manage what feels unmanageable. Oftentimes they just go numb. Or they dissociate; they disappear on the inside.

Recovery from the ACoA trauma syndrome is all about reclaiming the fragmented parts of self that are trapped in another psychological and emotional time and place and bringing them into the here and now. It is translating hidden emotion into words so that feelings can be processed, new insight and meaning can be gained, and experiences can be knitted back together with new understanding into a coherent and present-oriented picture of the functioning self and the self in relation to others. It is learning to live in the present rather than in the past or future.

This field has many pioneers whose remarkable sharing and collaborations over the years have lit a lamp for others to follow. Some of these pioneers are Margaret Cork, Claudia Black, Sharon Wegscheider-Cruse, Robert Ackerman, Jane Middleton-Moz, Stephanie Brown, Don Coyhis, Jerry Moe, Janet Woititz, Rokelle Lerner, Faye Calhoun, Jeannette Johnson, Phil Diaz, Patricia O'Gorman, Frances Brisbane, Stephanie Covington, Anna Whiting Sorrel, Hoover Adger, Lala Strassner, Cathleen Brooks Weiss, Ann Smith, Ellen Morehouse, Patrick Carnes, John Bradshaw, and Timmen Cermak.

Research on trauma made my own work come alive and provided a research base that began my own exploration of what I
call the ACoA Trauma Syndrome; much gratitude to Bessel van
der Kolk, Judith Hermann, and Lisa Najavitts for their seminal
work in this area. Another leg of the stool that the syndrome
stands on is attachment research, which I apply to my understanding of how childhood development is affected by growing
up with addiction. Those in the area of attachment by whom I
have been led are Maria Montessori, Jonathon Bowlby, D. W.
Winnicott, Alan Schore, Stanley Greenspan, and Daniel Siegel. Robert Anda's research on Adverse Childhood Experiences
(ACE) has elevated awareness and brought attention to the long-
term impact that growing up with addiction can have on both
mental and physical health, making an invaluable contribution
toward policy in this area.

Psychodrama is my method of treating people who have been
traumatized or people simply looking to increase their own level
of spontaneity, creativity, and aliveness. In this area I have been
most impacted by J. L. Moreno, Zerka Moreno, and Dr. Robert
Siroka, whose excellent training and vision for this method lit
my own healing spirit.

It is my hope that by the end of this book you will have an in-
depth understanding of trauma; it is also my hope that reading
this book will help to make trauma seem less strange and threatening to cope with and help you to develop various strategies
for lifestyles that both minimize its occurrence and intensity and
process it before it comes to have a life of its own. In Part 1, we
discuss and draw pictures of the black-and-white world of the

family system that contains addiction. In Part II, you will learn how your mind and body become affected and infected through living with the trauma-engendering dysfunctional relationship dynamics that surround addiction. In Part III, we explore case studies involving process addictions or the many forms of compulsive behaviors that self-medication can assume.

In Part IV, we'll take a step down the path of healing from the ACoA Trauma Syndrome and offer tips on attitude and lifestyle changes that build resilience and strength. In Part V, we'll look at ways of breaking the intergenerational chain of pain. We'll see how the past can be separated from the present so that we can live with mindful, positive purpose in the here and now.

Many who embrace recovery come to experience it as a journey of self-discovery, one of expansion into a new sense of self, self in relationships, and meaning and purpose in life. Many find that the promises of twelve step program do come true and they "do not regret nor wish to close the door" on their past, because through processing it, they have come to a deeper sense of aliveness and self-confidence. Or as Edmund Spenser wrote in *The Faeire Queene*, "For whatsoever from one place doth fall, Is with the tide unto an other brought: For there is nothing lost, that may be found, if sought."

PART I:

Origins of the ACoA Trauma Syndrome

Either we have hope within us or we don't.
It is a dimension of the soul, and it is not essentially
dependent on some particular observation of the heart.
It transcends the world that is immediately experienced and is
anchored somewhere beyond its horizons. Hope, in this deep sense, is
not the same as joy that things are going well, or the willingness to
invest in enterprises that are obviously headed for early success, but
rather an ability to work for something because it is good,
not just because it stands a chance to succeed. Hope is definitely not
the same thing as optimism. It is not the conviction that
something will turn out well, but the certainty that
something makes sense, regardless of how it turns out.
It is hope, above all, which gives us the strength to
live and continually try new things.

—Václav Havel, Author and Politician

ONE

Collateral Damage: Growing Up in the Force Field of Addiction

What we don't let out traps us. We think, No one else feels this way, I must be crazy. So we don't say anything. And we become enveloped by a deep loneliness, not knowing where our feelings come from or what to do with them. Why do I feel this way?

—Sabrina Ward Harrison, Artist and Author

W e're doing a great job of giving attention to addicts these days. The paparazzi are keeping scarved, hooded, and sunglassed celebrities on the front pages of newspapers and magazines, their hands outstretched to block the probing glare of cameras and careening, meddling microphones.

As they head to treatment.

It's easy to capture addiction's image. It wears a certain disheveled, hung-over look that we all recognize.

But no one is snapping many pictures of the people they left behind. The rest of the family.

Because how do you photograph a broken heart or a shattered self?

What happens to the kids, the wives, the husbands, and the parents whose lives are devastated by the disease of alcoholism/addiction? Those who are left dazed, numb, and in silent, secret pain because they've used up all of their resources—emotional, psychological, and financial—on getting the addict into treatment?

How do *they* get well? Is the fallout from living with addiction like inhaling years of secondary smoke? Are they somehow at risk too?

Probably. Especially impacted are children, whose personality development is affected by growing up around the dysfunctional, interpersonal relationship dynamics that surround addiction. These dynamics become incorporated into their concept of self and self in relationship and get played out when they become adult children of alcoholics/addicts (ACoAs) with partners and families of their own. Consider these statistics:

- One out of four children is a CoA.
- Fifty-five percent of all family violence occurs in alcoholic/ addicted homes.
- Incest is twice as likely among daughters and sons of alcoholics/addicts.
- Alcohol is a factor in 90 percent of all child abuse cases.
- ACoAs are four times more likely to become alcoholics/ addicts than the general population.

- 50 percent of ACoAs marry alcoholics.
- 70 percent of ACoAs develop patterns of compulsive behavior as adults. These may include abusive patterns with alcohol, drugs, food, sex, work, gambling, or spending.

That was the bad news; here's some good news. CoAs often develop valuable life skills that benefit them throughout their lives. They can become purposeful, strong, and resolute adults who are great at toughing it out and being creative, clever risk-takers. Because they've developed unique strengths while meeting the challenges of their childhoods, ACoAs often go on to become independent and resourceful adults. They are CEOs and entrepreneurs, teachers, philanthropists, and politicians, and they flood the helping professions. They can be tireless over-achievers. Yet, while CoAs and ACoAs are often full of talent, competence, and humor, they may find themselves marching double-time in life, fueled by a need to somehow right a childhood wrong, and they may pay a price for this both in physical health and comfort in relationships.

Birth of the ACoA Movement

Though it may be difficult for those who grew up later to imagine, until 1980 none of us who were ACoAs knew it. We just thought we were maybe a little more complicated, perhaps a little darker than some of our friends. Maybe we knew that our parents drank a bit too much alcohol—a way bit too much perhaps—but we didn't know that was anything but a childhood experience that should be "forgotten about." None of us really knew that it was a syndrome or that we'd been traumatized. We were clueless about the pain that we didn't feel a right to have. The trauma we were left with did not easily show itself. Sadness or fear might be hidden under a variety of veneers in the ACoA; not only the obvious hurt or angry face but also a less obvious sweet, wistful (if not vacant) smile. An ACoA might also be someone hiding behind a mask of feigned complacency and functioning while being good and quiet and productive.

When the ACoA syndrome was given a name and face, it allowed those of us who were still reverberating from the pain of growing up with addiction to finally "exhale." To everyone's amazement, ACoAs became a movement almost overnight (Wegscheider-Cruse 1980, Black 1981, Woititz 1983, Middlton-Moz 1985). Thousands upon thousands of us poured out of the woodwork, breaking our isolation and embarrassment to connect with others who might understand, encouraged by the fact that we were not alone, nor were we crazy to be carrying childhood scars well into adulthood. We were ACoAs; we had a name. And there were a lot of us. A whole lot. We cried, felt our anger, met our heretofore-banished "inner children," and told them they could stop hiding. And we came to feel a renewed sense of hope and empowerment. Perhaps if we could know what was wrong with us, we might have a chance at correcting it.

Today we know that ACoAs' reaction to living in a chaotic environment, this unrelenting "waiting for the other shoe to drop," for life to rupture or betray us all over again, actually has a name: it's *hypervigilance,* and it is part of a syndrome called post-traumatic stress disorder (PTSD). When a person is unable to get away from a highly stressful situation—that is, if their survival urge to flee toward safety is thwarted—they are more likely to develop PTSD than if they can discharge their physiological urge to run or protect themselves. Those of us who grew up with addiction fit this description perfectly. How could we flee from our own homes? Where would we go? And the very people we wanted to flee from were our parents who we needed and loved. The very people who we would have gone to for love, understanding, and protection were the ones who were traumatizing us. Our parents yelled, raged, or passed out in front of us, and we stood there frozen in fear, like deer in the headlights, revved up for fight or flight but unable to move a muscle.

But the feelings we stuffed did not disappear. Our mind/body held onto them in a quivering silence. When ACoAs get triggered as adults, we return to those feelings and the mind/body we lived in at those childhood moments (van der Kolk 1994). We stand there, stress chemicals coursing through our bodies, looking like grown-ups but feeling on the inside like helpless, frightened children. Naming and defining the ACoA syndrome gave us a way to finally understand ourselves, to feel our way out of our frozenness so that we could finally grow up on the inside.

Many of us became deeply empowered by the ACoA movement. And many of us have made it our life's work to develop theory and research that flesh out exactly what it is that happens to the body, mind, and hearts of children who grow up with addiction and with the dysfunction and mental illness that are its constant bedfellows. The work that we have done over the past thirty years has moved from instinct and intuition to some of the most exciting research to emerge in the mental health field. Studies on trauma, neurobiology, and attachment, have more or less proven what we were beginning to understand from our clinical observation: that the shocking, humiliating, and debilitating experiences that accompany living with addiction do, in fact, literally shape our neural networks. And that the personality complications caused by this early pain and stress can and often do emerge years and years after the original trauma. This is what the ACoA movement was all about; a post-traumatic stress reaction. Long after children leave their alcoholic homes, they remain ensnared in repeating relationship patterns that are the direct result of having been traumatized in childhood. Old pain keeps remerging in new relationships. The names and relationships may have changed, but the pain is always the same.

Those of us who work in the field see daily that this problem has only gotten bigger. And because it has only gotten bigger, many of us feel that it is time to reintroduce these concepts to the general public. We have come a very long way in our understanding of this syndrome and our ability to treat it. Studies on resilience have even taught us to value many of the adaptive qualities that ACoAs develop along the way, such as inventiveness, creativity, and humor (Wolin and Wolin 1993) as well as how CoAs learn to mobilize support within their young worlds so that they can thrive (Luthar 2006, Yates 2003). With a deeper understanding of ACoA issues, trauma, and neurobiology, we are much better able to help people recover from it than we were when this movement began.

Three Types of ACoAs

In my experience, there are three types of ACoAs. The first type seems to feel that their alcoholic home did not affect them all that much and since they are no longer living in it, they are fine. This group can be rather oblivious to the impact that they are having on those around them. They tend to act out their unresolved pain in controlling, enmeshing, or even abusive ways and to have either overly intense emotional reactions or suspiciously low levels of reaction, having developed a pattern in childhood of alternating between intense emotional states and shutting down.

The second type of ACoAs are fairly aware but don't truly want to do the tough emotional work it will take to really deal with the pain they carry; it makes them feel too vulnerable and helpless to experience those difficult emotions, and/or they feel disloyal breaking the family "secret" that all was not so perfect. These AcoAs are confusing to be close to. They sound like they understand what dynamics may be at play in difficult interactions but they go back and forth in terms of changing their own behavior. They give enough "insight" to make you want to come back for more but not enough behavior change so you can really relax.

The third type wants to look at their past and are willing to do the work that it takes to do so. They learn to be different on the inside and they experience enormous bursts of passion, creativity, and energy as they free up emotional, psychological, and physiological frozenness. They make significant personal changes that also translate into interpersonal changes. They may still be affected by their past but they know what to do when their feelings become stormy and their self-esteem takes a hit. They can adopt healthy ways of managing life circumstances. This group often comes to feel grateful for a painful past as it leads them to an enhanced awareness of life and love; they often report a deepened ability to engage with life, relationships, and their own spiritual path.

Defining the ACoA Trauma Syndrome

The ACoA trauma syndrome is a post-traumatic stress syndrome in which suppressed pain from childhood reemerges and is experienced, re-created, and lived out in adulthood. It is the direct result of growing up with the traumatizing dynamics of addiction or adverse childhood experiences (Anda 2006). Years and years after leaving their addicted homes, ACoAs carry the pain of their past relationships into their partnering, parenting, and workplaces. Childhood feelings that were never identified, worked through, and understood get triggered and projected into their adult relationships or sink into the body, where they increase chances of many illnesses from hypertension to heart disease. (Anda 2006). But often, ACoAs don't know why any of this is happening or that it's happening at all. Years after the stressor has been removed they live, in a way, as if it were still there (van der Kolk 1987). Years after they have left their childhood living rooms, developed careers, married, and had their own children, they remain hypervigilant: they wait for the other shoe to drop, for the people they love to betray, hurt, or humiliate them all over again. They carry their living rooms with them. When triggered, the present dissolves and gives way to "remembrances of things past," and suddenly, they are that hurt child all over again, frozen in place, not knowing what to say or do to bring this childhood "feeling state" into adult intelligence and language. They're trapped in an immature feeling state that belongs to a different time and place, but the unfelt needs, resentments, and wounds seem very real and about the present. And because they are in that state, they read the person or situation that triggered them as, in a sense, bigger than they are. They have little or no awareness of how their wounds from the past may be bleeding into their present. And possibly their future.

It is a cruel reality that the craziness, the sick and twisted emotional and psychological patterns of the addict, can be contagious. You cannot live with this illness without catching it. Psyches, brains, and neurological systems are built to be porous and adaptive. Our neurological networks are shaped by those we are raised by; who *they* are seamlessly becomes who we are through neurological patterning. Phenomena like limbic resonance or mirror neurons (Rizzolatti, Fabbri-Destro, and Cattaneo 2009) are being increasingly understood by research. We are actually biologically wired to pick up on and incorporate the rhythms and behaviors of others so we can learn habits, experience others empathically, and feel deeply connected. This is part of the phenomenon of attachment; we need to have the capacity to attach between parent and child and partner and to pair bond so that we can raise children successfully into adulthood. These emotional patterns are wired into us by nature, no longer nature vs. nuture; research reveals that both form the brain/body templates from which we feel and behave. This deep attachment cuts both ways. It means that we share our joys and pains and help each other through them; it also means that the thinking, feeling, and behavior of a disease like addiction gets "caught" and mirrored by the whole family.

The War at Home

Research on Vietnam veterans has revealed how trauma from a past, relatively short period of time can hold soldiers—and, effectively, all the people around them—hostage for the rest of their lives. Though most soldiers make a successful readjustment according to research, there is a significant group who continue to exhibit signs of post-traumatic stress. Left unchecked, psychological wounds related to post-traumatic stress disorder (PTSD) can alter a soldier's temperament and leave him with problems such as generalized anxiety, depression, occupational instability, marital conflicts, and family problems. Moreover, veterans with PTSD are more likely to report marital, parental, and other family adjustment problems (including violence) than veterans without PTSD (Jordan et al. 1992). This is a phenomenon that can cause large psychic wounds of war to reemerge at a later date long after the war is over. This reliving and re-creation of past pain in present-day relationships is what a post-traumatic stress reaction is all about. The soldier coping with PTSD might rage or become violent with his spouse or children because violence has become, we might say, part of his psyche and his nervous system. He might withdraw into a preoccupied, confused world of his own because he knows no other way of managing his huge emotions or his paradoxically flat, shutdown inner world. He cycles back and forth between unregulated extremes, moving from numbness to rage in literally the blink of an eye. He may turn to drugs or alcohol or sexual acting out to medicate the emotional pain and flashbacks that burden and disturb him. Not surprisingly, the soldiers who are the most vulnerable for developing PTSD from war are those who experienced childhood trauma in the home (Kulka et al. 1990a, Kulka et al. 1990b).

For the past three decades, the mental health field has been witnessing similar symptoms in those who grew up with adverse childhood experiences (Anda 2006) such as abuse, neglect, and particularly, addiction in the home. The phenomenon of adult children of alcoholics and addicts reveals its own version of pain from one part of life emerging long after the "war" is over. Children who grew up with adverse childhood experiences, who could not express or even experience their own emotional pain because their circumstances did not allow for it, may re-create in their adult relationships the painful experiences from their primary relationships in childhood.

On the outside, ACoAs often have things well under control. On the inside, however, they may experience a low hum of negative feelings about the self, such as insecurity, inadequacy, phoniness, unlovableness, anxiety, or confusion. In times of chaos and crisis, ACoAs can be very composed and function well but they may have trouble when things go normally, too slowly, are not under their control, don't go their way, or don't go as they expect. (Woititz 1983).

ACOoAs and Intimacy

Soldiers who have PTSD may duck at the sound of a car backfiring, unconsciously fearing that it is the sound of gunfire. Even though they are no longer anywhere near a battlefield, they carry the scars and the fear that make that loud sound still feel threatening.

For ACoAs the battlefield is oftentimes intimate relationships, and the loud sounds or triggers can be as innocuous as a fight in the next room, a sudden change of mood, or a tense or aggressive vocal tone. Because they were traumatized in their home and by the people who they loved and depended on for care, nurturance, and even basic survival, ACoAs' fear and hypervigilance tend to reemerge when they create families of their own. Intimate relationships such as partnering, and parenting are common ACoA triggers that reactivate childhood fears. As adults, when we encounter situations that feel similar to ones we experienced as kids, our fear gets triggered but we don't really understand why because we never figured it out in the first place. We go back into a state of hyperarousal and hypervigilance and all of the tangled mess of confused and conflicting feelings we experienced as kids seem to swarm around our heads but we don't know what got us there or how to get out of it. Often, we erroneously link our feelings of fear to whatever is around us at the moment. Actually, it isn't so much those situations in and of themselves that are scaring us; we're afraid that those situations will trigger unconscious and unprocessed feelings that we won't be able to handle or make sense of. Beneath the level of our conscious awareness, we become a scared child all over again. Triggered by something that reminds us of a time in our lives when we might have felt helpless, scared, and vulnerable, we become lost in a wordless web of unprocessed or disequilibrating emotions, not knowing how to sort them out or come back from them. Many adults when in this state do what they did as kids: they freeze like a deer in the headlights; they try to become "invisible" until their feeling of danger passes. It is part of the natural fear response: if no one sees me, no one will hurt me.

How many times have I heard clients describe themselves as having felt invisible in their own homes? Was it that no one saw them, or did they find home a scary place? Were they invisible, or were they frozen in fear and experiencing themselves as "disappeared"? Still another part of the trauma response is aggression or withdrawal: triggered ACoAs may either intimidate people or avoid them in an attempt to avoid feeling vulnerable.

Of course these same intimate relationships can be the ACoA's path to healing as they learn to back up when triggered and understand that within those triggered memories is the key to their unlocking and understanding just what hurt them most.

When Pain Goes Underground

Think of it this way: you're a seven-year-old kid in a home where Dad gets drunk and rages. Mom stands, exhausted, and tries to protect you some of the time, gives up and hides in her room some of the time, and joins Dad in raging some of the time. You, the kid, are scared and quite trapped: you can't really run away; this is home after all. If you talk back—or worse, try to fight—you might get hit or sent to your room, or worst of all, made to stay and live through one of those humiliating, soul-pounding lectures about how bad you are. Or you might get ignored and feel yourself literally dissappearing. So you feel helpless and you sort of collapse and go numb. Or you freeze, you "go away" somewhere into your imagination while your body still stands there.

In this scene, there is a power imbalance for sure, and you're at the short end of it. You have little access to outside sources of support; you are, after all, only seven. And the person or people you would generally go to for comfort and solace are the ones who are hurting you. All of these factors make this a traumatizing moment for a child. And to add to it, you are making sense of it all through the eyes of a seven-year-old. You may wonder, as children do, what went wrong and how to fix it. You may feel inept at helping or blame yourself. So you can feel not only hurt but also confused, responsible, at fault, and unable to do anything about it. In other words, you feel helpless. And you may not have people you can go to for a quick "reality check." So you swallow this scene whole. The picture gets frozen right there, and so do the feelings surrounding it . . . and that picture doesn't necessarily change much over time. It lives inside the psyche where it becomes double- and triple-exposed with other similar pictures, and many of these scenes get blended together in a sort of inner portrait of the self and the self in relationship.

Later, these "inner pictures" get played out in our adult relationships. They template further experience. (So do the good pictures, by the way; they just don't give us as many problems so we don't worry about them). This is the dilemma of the ACoA, the dilemma that we will explore in more depth throughout this book.

Leaching and Leaking of Buried Pain

When we grow up and have families and relationships of our own, those inner pictures of the self and the self in relationship reemerge. Neatly filed feelings, actions, and imagery that we imagined were well hidden fly out of their envelopes and folders straight into and onto everyone's faces. And those pictures have incredible detail. It is amazing just how carefully the unconscious records, remembers, and re-creates what has gone before. A random familiar smell, texture, or a few bars of music and we sail back into a forgotten moment of time in the blink of an eye. Past becomes prologue. At that moment when we are triggered, we become trapped by our own unresolved history and set up to repeat it. Though we may occupy an adult body, we return to this child-place inside of ourselves. In addition to the psychological and emotional bind we may find ourselves in when we're triggered, our bodies are also reliving the trauma. Our breath gets short, our hearts may pound, our stomachs flip-flop, our throat goes dry, and our muscles tense up. We feel helpless and unable to make decisions all over again. In this way, the ACoA trauma syndrome involves both the body and mind and healing from it is a mind/body process.

Recovering from PTSD is just as important as recovering from addiction and needs to be taken just as seriously. ACoAs need to sober up emotionally and psychologically so they do not live out the sort of "dry drunk" patterns that mirror addiction-related thinking, feeling, and behavior, even when alcohol and drugs are not in the picture. Trauma and PTSD invariably become intergenerational. Even if the ACoA or traumatized adult does not become an addict (though many do), he or she passes on the kind of emotional and psychological thinking, feeling, and behavior that can engender trauma, addiction, and dysfunction in subsequent generations.

TWO

The Making of an ACoA:
Living Behind a Mask

You could have all the crazy thoughts you wanted,
as long as you smiled and kept them to yourself.

—Maqra Purnhagen, *Past Midnight*

L iving in an alcoholic family system is like driving at night without your headlights on—you are always squinting to see a little
better, wondering what lies ahead in the road or what might jump
out at you from behind the bushes.

Visit the living room of the average family that is "living
with"—or should I say "living in"—addiction, and you are likely
to find a family that is clinging to its own emotional edges, one
that's functioning in emotional, psychological, and behavioral
extremes. A family in which small things that might otherwise
be solved smoothly become bigger than necessary or blow up
and turn into minor catastrophes, while outrageous, self-destructive, or even abusive behavior may go entirely ignored and unaddressed. Where feelings can get very big, very fast, or literally
disappear into nowhere with equal velocity. There can be a low

hum of apprehension surrounding even the smallest decisions, while major life decisions are barely focused on. A family where what doesn't matter can get a lot of emphasis while what does matter can get swept under the rug, shelved, circumvented, or downright denied. A family, in short, that doesn't know what "normal" is.

"All or nothing" characterizes the trauma-induced response. Those affected by trauma tend to go from 0–10 and 10–0 with no speed bumps in between. They have trouble living in 4, 5, and 6. Because they don't have healthy ways of finding an emotional middle ground, they achieve balance by shooting from one emotional extreme to the other, over- or underresponding, and zooming right past middle ground as if it weren't even there. They have trouble with self-regulation. They have trouble "staying present" or "in their bodies" and integrating thought with feeling; they live in their heads or in their feelings. This is part of why those within the family don't learn what "normal" is; it reflects the loss of neuromodulation that can accompany trauma.

The "All or Nothing" Character of Our Response to Trauma

A hallmark characteristic of CoAs and ACoAs who have been traumatized by the effects of growing up with parental addiction is a loss of neuromodulation (van der Kolk 1986). Children learn the skills of self-regulation and balance in the arms of those who raise them. When the family atmosphere is full of mood swings that are rarely explained and put into an understandable framework, children are left to make sense of their surrounding circumstances with the immature reasoning of a child and to regulate their own moods in their own, childlike ways. Their thinking, feeling, and behavior all too often come to mirror what they see around them, and this is what they internalize as the norm.

Living with adults who cannot easily express and process emotion in healthy ways also leaves children to wonder about themselves as well as what is going on in the family. They sense that great wells of feelings exist but nothing is said out loud. Negative feelings leak out through criticism or withholding of affection. Children observe the sudden bursts of anger or tears that might indicate problems, but then all of those clues disappear into nowhere and no one talks about it or explains what they are feeling or thinking. In this environment, family members often develop the habit of hiding what they are feeling and not sharing what is going on inside of them, because sharing it gets them nowhere. Children in this atmosphere may come to feel anxious about their parents, their siblings, and themselves. As parents drop the ball, there are regular skirmishes among siblings for a sense of power and place. Siblings may turn to each other for support, but they also learn that they have to compete for the limited love and attention that their parents have to give. They may learn dysfunctional relationship habits such as manipulating parents to get what they need, jockeying for an edge over another sibling, or sidling up to one parent and taking sides against the other. Parents may co-opt one child as a surrogate partner and distance the other. Family factions, both overt and covert, can develop, creating an "in crowd" and an "out crowd." Thus, not only the emotional atmosphere of the family becomes thrown off, but the relationships within the family become distorted as well. In this environment, it can be a challenge for the growing child to find his or her own emotional and relational regulation and balance.

Most relationships have stormy moments; it's a natural and even healthy part of being alive, attached, adaptive, and growing. But alcoholic families get lost in the storm; they lose some of their ability to "right" themselves and find solid ground.

Fleeing on the Inside: When CoAs Dissociate

Picture again the child facing her drunk parent. She is short, he is tall. She thinks with a child's limited reasoning, he's been to college. She has her truck or teddy dangling from her arms. He is holding the keys to the house, the car, and credit cards. She could fight, but she knows that if she tries to stand up for herself, she will only come to her daddy's waist. She could flee, but where would she go in her footy pajamas with no money? So she does what she can do. She shuts up. She stands there like a little soldier and takes it. She freezes, holds her pain, hurt, and tension in the musculature of her little body and flees on the inside; she dissociates. Dissociation—or "fleeing on the inside"—can be hard to see. After all, your body is still there—you talk and interact, you seem to be there, but you are not in your own skin. You're not present. You're on autopilot. Life appears to be happening out there, somewhere, but you're not quite present.

Some of the factors that sear trauma in place and make it more likely that a CoA will develop post-traumatic trauma syndrome are:

Parent Is Causing the Stress

The same people who children would go to for comfort—their parents—are the ones hurting them. This is a double whammy for the children and makes abuse within the home all the more disempowering and debilitating.

Basic Power Imbalance

Children are trapped in a world created, run, and paid for by the parent, and they have limited access to other resources. If they fight back, they risk getting grounded, hit, or having their allowance taken away. Older siblings can also trap younger siblings in this power imbalance that can be part of a trauma bond. Being at the disempowered end of a trauma bond can mean that children are stuck going along, stuck saying yes even when they want to say no.

Lack of Access to Outside Sources of Support

Having somewhere to go that feels safe and offers a different model of how to live can have a lasting, positive impact on a child that counters the effects of growing up with trauma. ACoAs often talk about grandparents' houses, spending time at the neighbor's, the house of a friend or relative, or a job where they could regain their balance and recognize that the world is full of options. These experiences restore a sense of hope and direction for the CoA.

Developmental Level of the CoA

Psychological and emotional growth happen along a continuum. Children are always understanding their environment with the psychological equipment they have at any particular stage of development. Small children may come up with fantastical, magical solutions that are the product of their immature minds. They may learn to bend the truth, for example, to make it less frightening, creating "reasons" for their parents erratic behavior that are less threatening than the truth: "Daddy yells at me more because I am his favorite." As adolescents, they have a greater ability to perceive reality but are still in the throes of their own individuation. Adolescents may have trouble figuring out how to separate from a situation and hold onto a sense of self when the circumstances of the family already feel fundamentally abandoning and confusing. Young adults can also struggle with families who "fall apart." Once they leave, their home base disappears and is not there to return to.

Length of Time the CoA Spends in a Dissociated State

While dissociation may represent our best, albeit unconscious, attempt at managing the unmanageable when we were small and trapped, it can become a liability and is considered to be maladaptive if it becomes a pattern that we fall into without awareness. "Research tends to show," according to the International

Society for the Study of Trauma and Dissociation, "that dissocia-tion stems from a combination of environmental and biological factors. The likelihood that a tendency to dissociate is inherited genetically is estimated to be zero" (Simeon et al. 2001). While dissociation is most commonly the result of being in situations of physical or sexual abuse or neglect (Putnam 1985), dissocia-tion may also occur even when there has been no overt physi-cal or sexual abuse (Anderson and Alexander 1996; West, Adam, Spreng, and Rose 2001). "Children may become dissociative in families in which the parents are frightening, unpredictable, are dissociative themselves, or make highly contradictory communi-cations" (Blizard, 2001; Liotti, 1992, 1999a, b).

Too much time spent in a deeply dissociated state can con-tribute to PTSD. Additionally, lesser forms of dissociation can become an unconscious solution that can impair our ability to be "present" and to connect in other situations. For example, a child dissociating in a classroom where he's scared may be a child who has trouble paying attention. Or an adult who dissociates in an intimate relationship may not be present enough to truly live in the relationship and understand it.

Perceived or Real Helplessness

Living with the mood swings or the abuse, neglect, or emotional and physical violence that can accompany addiction is terrifying for children, and they can feel helpless to protect themselves or those close to them in the face of it. Learned helplessness can be part of the ACoA trauma syndrome. In disaster situations, the smallest form of involvement can allow victims to be less symptomatic. Even cleaning up branches and debris after a hurricane can allow those affected to restore a sense that they can do something to improve their situation, which counters the PTSD symptom of learned helplessness. Children can counter their own sense of helplessness by doing positive things for themselves, whether writing in a personal journal, helping to restore order in the house, engaging in fun or meaningful school activities that build their sense of having their own life, or getting a job to earn their own spending money.

Organic Make-Up of the CoA

Basic intelligence is a factor in resilience along with the child's own organic structure. Some children seem better equipped by nature to cope with adverse circumstances in spite of their gender or position in the family. Though it is virtually impossible to separate the combined effects of nature and nurture, there can be organic reasons that can influence a child's ability to cope with adversity effectively.

Length and Severity of the Stressor

The cumulative effect of childhood toxic stress is part of what gives the ACoA trauma syndrome teeth. And though toxic stressors are common throughout society, some are more devastating than others. When CoAs move into adulthood with a history of childhood trauma, they are more vulnerable to being traumatized as adults (Krystal 1968).

Lack of Access to Support Outside the Family

Children feel trapped by their families through both the bonds of love and attachment and the natural dependency of childhood. Generally speaking, the more dysfunctional a family becomes, the more isolated it becomes from other families. Children who have access to sources of support can be helped to build resilience that reduces the sense of being trapped and allows them to feel as if they can do something to help themselves.

Sensory Nature of the Stressor

The more senses that are involved and attached to experience, the more the brain and limbic system absorb and remember it. First responders at Ground Zero on 9/11 were more likely to become symptomatic because of the amount of sensory input they experienced; they saw, smelled, heard, touched, and tasted the scene and experienced powerful emotions of horror, disgust, fear, and compassion.

Home is a highly sensorial environment full of smells, sounds, touch, tastes, and imagery. What happens in the home is absorbed deeply into the brain and body.

False-Self Functioning

When we discover that being who we are does not get us what we need, we may learn to be who we aren't. When parents are not curious about their children's genuine feelings, giving them help in understanding them, children become less curious about their own feelings (Cozolino 2006). They may begin a pattern of hiding their authentic selves in favor of developing a self that is acceptable to the family.

Children with narcissistic parents may develop a false self around gratifying the needs and expectations of their narcissistic parents; they learn that to stay connected, parental needs and wants have to remain the primary focus. Addiction can mirror narcissism in that the needs of the addict become a primary concern.

The more fearful the family is of being "exposed," the less space there is for honest reactions. Honesty carries with it a tacit call to action, a call to come out of hiding and uncover problems. If the family does not want to do this, children need to come up with a way to stay connected that does not challenge the acceptable status quo, essentially presenting a "normal" family face to the world rather than allowing the chinks in the family armor to be revealed.

For CoAs, this may even feel like a clever solution to a very pressing problem. We may contort parts of our personality to "fit in" or to "get points" so that we can remain part of the family as it sees itself. If we step out and begin to point out inconsistencies, lies, and deceptions, we are telling the system it needs to change. We risk becoming the bad guy.

The real danger lies not in creating a mask or false self; we all do this to some extent or another. It's natural to cultivate a false self for social or professional reasons or even for protection, but CoAs may spend so much time functioning within these parameters that their sense of authenticity becomes compromised. The sad outcome, however, is that the false self becomes so well-constructed and adaptable—or garners so much acceptance, approval, or even power within the family that spawned it—that eventually the true self becomes lost to us (Horney 1950). We hide our true self so effectively that even we can't find it. The false self is meant to absorb or take the pain that the child finds too overwhelming. The false self is largely unconscious.

This false self is also sometimes seen as the "idealized self" (Horney 1950). We construct a version of self that is better, stronger, and more able to cope, a self that is less easily wounded or made anxious. We may even come to idealize our particular solution—for example, bullying becomes strength or manipulation becomes cleverness. The false self steps in like an actor on a stage, hiding our stammering and insecurity under a smoke screen of well-modulated behavior or disguising our anger and envy beneath a syrupy smile. The family payoff can be great. Because this self is essentially constructed to meet the needs of the family and make the system work, we can get a lot of recognition and even control through playing the role well, the role that the family has written.

But the more time we spend functioning through a false self, the more underexplored the authentic self becomes. Like a muscle that atrophies from lack of use, the authentic self does not get the practice in living and interacting that would allow it to strengthen and grow. So even though the false self is meant to protect the more vulnerable self, it actually has the effect of weakening it. When people who have become dependent on false-self functioning go into therapy or enter a 12-step program, they can go through a period of feeling very vulnerable and shaky because they are removing their coping strategy and exposing the pain underneath it. But over time, new healthy emotional habits get created, and new ways of healthy coping get practiced and adopted.

THREE

Family Dynamics: Living in Two Worlds

"I have come to suspect that life itself may be a spiritual practice. The process of daily living seems able to refine the quality of our humanity over time. There are many people whose awakening to larger realities comes through the experiences of ordinary life, through parenting, through work, through friendship, through illness, or just in some elevator somewhere."

—Rachael Naomi Remen

In a home where what is abnormal becomes the norm and what is normal can seem increasingly elusive, one learns not to be surprised by anything. The rules and routines in an alcoholic family are constantly in an unpredictable state of flux—that is, the same behavior that gets you applause one day gets you grounded the next. Identities, roles, and relationships can be unstable. They shift based on the moods and needs of the parent rather than the needs of the developing children or the family as a whole. CoAs live in two worlds, and the thinking, feeling, and behavior for each world can be radically different. For example, while Dad is on a binge, Mom and Lisa get so close. Mom leans on Lisa to help her with Danny, and Lisa and Mom become confidants and best buddies. Lisa shares Mom's thoughts, worries, and interests. Lisa feels important and needed and elevated above kid status. Danny gets to run a little wild when Dad isn't calling him on his behavior. Mom is "easier" and he gets away with more.

But when Dad sobers up, Mom and Dad get close again, and Lisa is now treated like a child. Suddenly Mom is telling her to do her homework and clean her room. And when Lisa asks Mom the same kinds of questions she asks when Dad's drinking, Mom shuts the door and tells her to mind her own business. Danny comes to Lisa for company and she doesn't even mind all that much; in fact, she comes to rely on his needing her—he helps to fill the now vacant space so she isn't so lonely.

Another scenario is when Mom is drunk. She spends most of her time in her bedroom, so the kitchen—usually a part of her domain—feels suddenly empty. But available. Charlie and Betsey can do almost anything they want during the day when Dad's at work. They have the run of the house; they pick up groceries "for Mom" and add cigarettes and beer whenever they feel like it. And they can smoke and drink in the basement because Mom never comes out of her room. And Dad spends more time at the office.

But when Mom gets sober for a week or two or three, suddenly the house feels completely different. No more beer or cigarettes, and credit card purchases are checked out.

Then there is the scenario of the functioning alcoholic, the one whose cocktail hour is sacrosanct, the one who has learned just how much drinking he or she can get away with during the week, on the weekends, and over family vacations. Or the pot smoker whose family feels like life doesn't quite get started, or the cocaine user whose behavior is erratic and scary and changeable. Maybe Dad exercises just enough, eats just enough, and socializes just enough to ameliorate some of the negative effects of daily alcohol. He has the family well trained to not talk about how frustrated or worried they are, how Dad's health issues are cropping up, or how his time with the family just feels sort of . . . affected. These more hidden forms of addiction can be very hard on family members. Their perception that something is off or missing is never validated, and they are left to doubt themselves, which leads to anxiety.

When a substance or compulsive behavior rules family dynamics, family gravity gets thrown off kilter: sometimes it pulls too hard and we can't escape; sometimes it barely holds us in place. Kids learn to manoeuver in and out of their parents' moods, which rule the atmosphere, so CoAs become parentified children—little caretakers who from a young age learn how to manage problem adults. Or they have to develop a premature "independence" before they are ready and they do not learn how to reach out and get help with their normal developmental problems. And they can feel helpless and despondent, unable to do anything that can really lead to their family getting better, happier, or safer. CoAs develop a sixth sense of when to hide, when to run, and when to hurl themselves straight into the breach and bring their parent—who is whirling out of control—back from wherever they have gone. They become little soldiers of fortune—determined, committed, and filled with zealous love—but their battleground is the home where they live, and the fortune they seek is a smile and warm touch from a depressed mother, the goodness and strength returning to their drunk father, or the magic of a quiet evening at home just being, hanging out, and doing lots of sweet, normal nothing.

CoAs who repeatedly find themselves "alone" to manage situations that they experience as difficult or confusing may learn some bad lessons, and miss learning some good ones. These lessons may include:

- Emotional hiding: They learn to hide what they are really feeling.
- Unconscious emotional defenses: They learn not to feel, to numb out, or to split off/dissociate from pain.
- Semiconscious defenses: They learn to minimize, deny, or intellectualize problems rather than deal with them openly and directly.
- Projection of feelings: They learn to make their pain about someone or something else, just as their parent does.
- Relational fear or mistrust: They learn that love, need, and dependency can lead to pain.

The good lessons CoAs may not learn include:

- How to regulate their emotions by translating feelings into words and talking them out rather than acting them out.
- How to move away from feeling helpless, frightened, and overwhelmed and toward feeling re-empowered, centered, and balanced without self-medicating.

- How to work things out with another person in healthy ways so both people get to feel good again.

CoAs may also develop unusual strengths at an early age. The good lessons CoAs may learn include:

- How to manage frightening situations and keep their cool.
- How to have compassion for the suffering of others.
- How to tolerate pain and fear and continue to mush on in spite of the pain and fear in their own lives.
- How to be self-reliant and take bold action on behalf of themselves and others.
- How to come up with creative solutions to problems.
- How to trust their own "guts" and follow their own instincts.
- How to see the silver lining in a situation.
- How to reach out to others for help and support.
- That life can be challenging and disappointing but still wonderful.

ACoAs can be remarkably creative and interesting people; managing unmanagability from such a young age helps them develop some serious competence at it. They know a lot about plowing through and doing what needs to be done and coming up with original and unusual strategies to get things accomplished, and they can have a pretty side-splitting sense of humor while doing it. Additionally, ACoAs who learn to forgive and trust again have a kind of acceptance about life that is inspiring and motivating. One that can lead to deep happiness and vitality.

ACOA Survey: Positive and Negative ACoA-related Qualities

Following is a graph representing the choices made in a survey of 333 self-identified ACoAs. The bars on this survey represent the top ten characteristics (both negative and positive) ACoAs identified with the most in order of identification. This survey represents a random sampling of people who elected to take it. The population was drawn from readers of my blog on *Huffington Post, Recovery View,* and from my own students and clients in recovery. The survey was entirely anonymous; no personal identification was recorded.

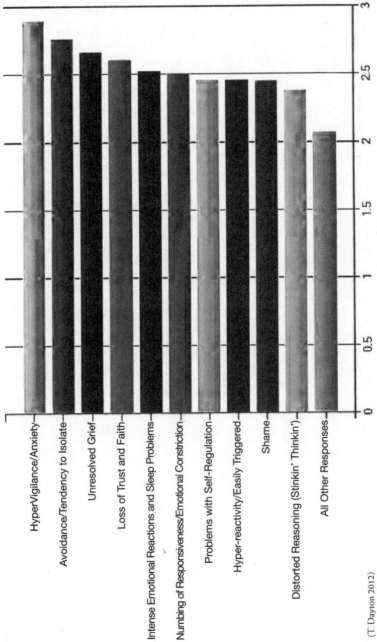

(T. Dayton 2012)

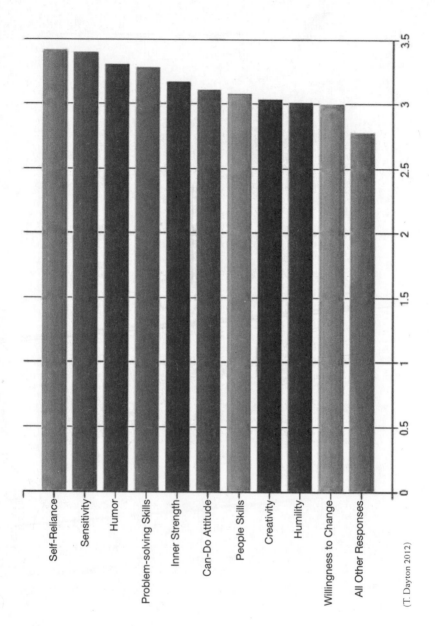

(T. Dayton 2012)

PART II:

Neurobiology of the ACoA Trauma Syndrome

"You did not ask to be born, but you are here. You have weaknesses as well as strengths. You have both because in life there is two of everything. Within you is the will to win, as well as the willingness to lose. Within you is the heart to feel compassion as well as the smallness to be arrogant. Within you is the way to face life as well as the fear to turn away from it. . . .
Being strong means taking one more step toward the top of the hill, no matter how weary you may be. It means letting the tears flow through the grief. It means to keep looking for the answer, though the darkness of despair is all around you. Being strong means to cling to hope for one more heartbeat, one more sunrise. Each step, no matter how difficult, is one more step closer to the top of the hill. To keep hope alive for one more heartbeat at a time leads to the light of the next sunrise, and the promise of a new day. The weakest step toward the top of the hill, toward sunrise, toward hope, is stronger than the fiercest storm. Keep going."

A Lakota Sioux grandfather to his grandson
from *Keep Going: The Art of Perseverance* by Joseph M. Marshall III

FOUR

Breaking Trust:
Stress and Rupture
in Family Bonds

What you leave behind is not what is engraved on stone
monuments but what is woven into the lives of others.

—Pericles

L ove and attachment are the primary forces that ensure life;
without these powerful mind/body drives, none of us would
be here. How we learn to love in our early relationships forms
the template for how we love throughout our lives.

Much of our brain and neurological development takes place
outside of the womb after birth and continues throughout childhood through the parent/child relationship. The endless tiny
communications and collaborations between parent and child,
each cuddle and coo, actually shapes our brains and our nervous
systems. Children do not have the capacity to regulate their own
emotions but depend on an "external regulator," such as the parent, to woo them back to a sense of balance when they become

distressed (Greenspan 2000). When a child becomes agitated, she has an inborn instinct to reach for her parent to lift her up and rock her back into a state of regulation, to soothe her stressed little nervous system, and help her to restore emotional balance.

"The child's first relationship, the one with the mother or father, acts as a template, as it permanently molds the individual's capacities to enter into all later emotional relationships," says Alan Schore, assistant clinical professor in the Department of Psychiatry and Biobehavioral Sciences at the UCLA School of Medicine (Schore 1991). As the parent interacts with the child, the child learns the skills of relating and self-regulation.

According to Schore, when the portions of the brain responsible for attachment and emotional control are not sufficiently stimulated during infancy because the infant is neglected, these sections of the brain will not develop properly. This can result in a child who is impulsive, emotionally unattached, or possibly even violent. The sensitivity and responsiveness of a parent actually stimulates and shapes the nerve connections in key sections of the brain responsible for closeness, attachment, emotional regulation, and well-being.

How We Absorb and Develop
Skills of Self-Regulation

Discussions on parenting these days circulate less around what parents do to children and more around how parents are with them. The "space" between parent and child is what really counts.

Sound emotional and psychological development are now under-stood to be related to the quality of the connectedness, attun-ement, and continuous interaction between the child and his or her primary caretakers. "Our nervous systems," says scientist Dan-iel Stern, "are constructed to be captured by the nervous systems of others, so that we can experience others as if from within their skin" (Stern 2010). This is our biological basis for empathy and emotional connection. Nature designed us to have this emotional attunement so that we can fit into the clan effectively and effi-ciently picking up on signals from those around us, adjusting our behavior and adapting it accordingly.

A baby's head is far too large to make it through a mother's pel-vis at birth; consequently, much of our brain growth (and hence brain/body neurological growth) takes place outside the womb throughout infancy and childhood. Children are born into this world only partially hardwired by nature for self-regulation; nur-ture does the rest. Through each tiny, soothing interaction with caregivers, children absorb the skills of self-regulation from their mothers and fathers and internalize them as their own. Children internalize and incorporate regular routines, a calm environment, and a soothing touch and voice, and all of these sense experiences sink into the child's limbic system and their body clock. Through the acquisition of these actual experiences of self regulation, a child is able to learn to regulate their emotions and other basic functions such as mood, appetite, libido, sleep, motivation, and capacity for bonding. These skills of emotional/self-regulation are what allow us to move from extremes in thinking, feeling, and behavior toward balance in all of these areas. (Schore 1994).

Parents instinctively rock, coo, cuddle, and sing to their children to help them to feel safe and calm. When children are distressed, being held and reassured allows them to internalize the felt sense of tolerating or "living through" overwhelming emotions until calm is restored. Over time, children internalize the ability to "hold" their own, powerful emotions; in other words, they develop the skills of emotional regulation.

Nature Favors Connection Over Disconnection

Touch is the language of childhood. Parents and children who are held in a mutual embrace each experience that magic sensation of body chemicals that calm and nourish. Touching our children is like watering a plant; touch releases oxytocin—nature's "brain fertilizer"—into their bloodstreams and, as a bonus, into the parent's bloodstream as well. Touch also floods the child's and the parent's body with serotonin, the body's natural antidepressant that soothes and regulates moods. "Hugs and kisses during these critical periods make . . . neurons grow and connect properly with other neurons," writes Dr. Arthur Janov in his book *The Biology of Love* (2000). These hugs and kisses not only nourish the body of the child so that he or she can grow properly but they simultaneously nourish the parent's body. Both are calmed and soothed. It is physically and emotionally heart smart, good for the body, the emotions, the soul, and the soul of the relationship. Nature rewards caring and close connection with body chemicals that make us feel good and punishes disconnection by flooding our bodies with uncomfortable stress hormones that make us feel bad, like cortisol. Alan Schore has demonstrated that cortisol, which floods the brain during intense crying and other stressful events, actually destroys nerve connections in critical portions of an infant's developing brain (1991). Evolution ensures, through the chemicals of connection, that parents and children maintain sufficiently powerful and close bonds so that children will make it safely to adulthood. And it uses chemicals of *disconnection* to seal the bargain. Abandonment hurts.

Child researcher Megan Gunnar and her colleagues found that three-month-old infants who received consistent responsive care produced less cortisol than infants who had received less responsive care. When tested again at age two, children who were classified as insecurely attached continued to show elevated levels of cortisol, continued to fall into the less securely attached group, and appeared more fearful and inhibited than their more securely attached counterparts. Dr. Gunnar's findings reveal that the level of stress experienced in infancy permanently shapes the stress responses in the brain, which then affect memory, attention, and emotion (Gunnar et al 1996; Gunnar 1998). Babies and toddlers may be better off with plenty of closeness and touching; like little puppies, they want to be on top of each other, and like all animals, they feel more secure and even learn valuable social skills through this interactive touching and play (Panksepp 2003).

Effects of Childhood Stress

Understanding the nature of these powerful attachment bonds helps us to wrap our minds around why the threat of rupture between parent and child, which is an ever-present concern of the CoA, causes such stress. Addicts abandon their children whether they love them or not; when they are in the throes of using, their substance comes first. Because parent/child bonds are survival bonds, threatening them through the trauma of neglect, mental illness, addiction, or divorce can cause us to experience that rupture as traumatic. Children want to stay close to their parents and may even join their parents in a compulsive habit (process addiction) such as overeating so they don't feel on the "outside" of a behavior that disturbs, confuses, or abandons them.

Rejection can actually hurt physically. We use words like "broken heart" or "heartache" to describe the physical pain of rejection. "Social rejection activates the very zones of the brain that generate, among other things, the sting of physical pain . . . our brain's pain centers may have taken on a hypersensitivity to social banishment because exclusion was a death sentence in human prehistory" (Eisenberger, Lieberman, and Williams 2003).

We are wired to want to imitate, model, and belong. When children of alcoholics/addicts fear abandonment by their primary caretakers, they can feel that their very lives are at stake.

Long-Term Effects of Toxic Stress During Childhood

The Adverse Childhood Experiences (ACE) study is one of the largest studies ever conducted on the relationship between maltreatment in childhood and long-term effects on health and well-being, and it tells us much about the CoA experience. The ACE study is a collaboration between the Centers for Disease Control Prevention and Kaiser Permanente, an integrated managed-care consortium based in San Diego, California. The ACE study found that the risk factors that constitute "toxic stress" and contribute to long-term physical, emotional, and psychological health were surprisingly common. The 2006 study, led by Robert F. Anda, MD, MS, and David W. Brown, DSc, MScPH, MSc, included more than 17,000 health maintenance organization (HMO) members who underwent a comprehensive physical examination that provided detailed information about their childhood experiences of abuse, neglect, and family dysfunction. This study quantifies the long-term effects of cumulative childhood toxic stress from growing up with addiction and/or other types of adverse experiences during childhood.

The researchers were not looking toward family addiction as a unique risk factor in their study design. Rather, parental addiction and the dysfunctional behaviors that clustered around it kept emerging through the collection of data as one of the statistically most significant causes of mental, emotional, and physical health problems in adulthood. People with high ACE scores who experienced the cumulative effect of growing up with a cluster of adverse childhood experience tended to be those who fell into the health-care and penal systems in adulthood because their childhood stress was more than their brain/body could process. And the people who might have helped them to ameliorate their stress were often the ones causing it, or they were too overwhelmed with their own stress to be helpful to their children.

Why Childhood Stress Has a Long-Term Effect

Dr. Anda describes why ongoing, traumatic experiences such as growing up with addiction, abuse, or neglect in the home can have such tenacious effects. "For an epidemic of influenza, a hurricane, earthquake, or tornado, the worst is quickly over; treatment and recovery efforts can begin. In contrast, the chronic disaster that results from ACEs is insidious and constantly rolling out from generation to generation." If the effects of toxic stress are not understood so that children can receive some sort of understanding and support from home, school, and community, these children simply "vanish from view . . . and randomly reappear—as if they are new entities—in all of your service systems later in childhood, adolescence, and adulthood as clients with behavioral, learning, social, criminal, and chronic health problems" (Anda, Felitti, et al. 2006).

ACEs Are Common

Contrary to the myth that adverse childhood experiences do not happen as frequently in middle- or upper-middle-class homes, toxic ACEs occur regularly and throughout all social classes and races. Dr. Anda feels that society "has bought into a set of misconceptions." Some of those myths are that "(1) ACEs are rare, (2) that they happen somewhere else, (3) that they are perpetrated by monsters, (4) that some, or maybe most, children can escape unscathed, or if not, (5) that they can be rescued and healed by emergency response systems" (ibid).

In the ACE study, 94 percent of those studied had gone to college and lived in San Diego, a very nice and not inexpensive area to live in, and had access to excellent health care. But even in this population, adverse childhood experiences were common.

The ten Adverse Childhood Experiences studied were:

- Childhood abuse
- Emotional/physical/sexual abuse
- Emotional or physical neglect
- Growing up in a seriously dysfunctional household as evidenced by witnessing:
  —Domestic violence
  —Alcohol or other substance abuse in the home
  —Mentally ill or suicidal household members
  —Parental marital discord (as evidenced by separation or divorce)
  —Having a household member imprisoned (ibid)

Adverse Childhood Experiences
Don't Occur in Isolation

If a CoA grows up with addiction, that is probably not the only risk factor in the home. ACEs tend to cluster; once a home environment

is disordered, the risk of witnessing or experiencing emotional, physical, or sexual abuse rises dramatically. Anda and his team learned
that ACEs tend to occur several at a time. CoAs are statistically likely
to also have several other co-occurring issues from the above list. For
example, addiction is statistically likely to be accompanied by abuse,
neglect, or emotional, physical, or sexual abuse.

High Cost of Ignoring Family Pain

In a recent edition of *Addiction Report*, researchers report that
family members of alcohol and drug patients had higher average
costs per member-month and average overall costs, including psychiatric and alcohol and drugs, AOD than control family members;
they also had almost five times higher psychiatry/AOD costs and
more than twice the ER cost. For both groups, more than 40 percent of total costs were attributable to in-patient stays" (Weisner,
Parthasarathy, Moore, and Martens 2010).

According to Lewis D. Eigen of the National Association of
for Children of Alcoholic (NACoA), "This means that a family of
four would have $40,000 in excess medical costs from illnesses and
emergency room visits. These do *not* include other social service
costs, social welfare costs, law enforcement, education, and the
like. Also, the costs are in constant dollars, so if there is typical
inflation, the numbers would be larger. Historically, with medi-
cal inflation, we are looking at about $80,000 over a twenty-year
span. Sis Wenger, NACoA's CEO reflects that "We cannot afford
to ignore the problems of CoAs, either financially or morally."

Dealing with Toxic Stress

Dr. Anda refers to "dose and effect"; the more numerous the toxic stress clusters, the more serious and long term the effect and the higher the chance of getting involved in alcohol or drug use. There is also a higher risk for other issues, including having risky sexual behavior; STDs; contracting HIV from injected drug use; suffering from pulmonary disease; smoking-related lung disease; autoimmune disease; poor adolescent health; teen pregnancy; and mental health issues. There is also a higher risk of revictimization, instability of relationships, and poor performance in the workforce.

To deal with what constitutes a national health crisis, we need to reduce the toxic stress load on our developing children. It is very expensive to help people who fall into the healthcare system and the judicial system and improve their outlook once the effects of toxic stress have set in. Much simpler and less expensive is to change our parenting and educational practices and reduce the effects of toxic stress on the developing child. Rather than wait for diseases to develop and then address them one at a time in adulthood, Anda feels that we need to look at the child-rearing practices that create the kind of toxic stress that undermines long term health and resilience (Anda, Felleti, et al. 2006). The kind of toxic stress that pounds away at our autoimmune system in childhood and all too often results in fully developed disorders as adults.

No situation need be inherently traumatic. How we experience the circumstances of our lives determines whether or not we find them traumatizing. The presence of caring adults who help children decode the ever-unfolding situations of their worlds is a great protective buffer for the child. Without this reassuring presence, the child has no way of knowing whether or not to be scared, or how scared to be.

FIVE

Living on Our Emotional Edges: The Mind/Body Impact of Trauma

I became what I am today at the age of twelve, on a frigid overcast day in the winter of 1975. I remember the precise moment, crouching behind a crumbling mud wall, peeking into the alley near the frozen creek. That was a long time ago, but it's wrong what they say about the past, I've learned, about how you can bury it. Because the past claws its way out. Looking back now, I realize I have been peeking into that deserted alley for the last twenty-six years.

—Khaled Hosseini, *The Kite Runner*

Imagine that you're walking through the woods on a sunny, crisp, spring day. The pleasant songs of birds are floating through the morning air. Your head is filled with the intoxicating scents of spring and you feel bathed by warm, caressing breezes. You're relaxed, at ease, and wandering through your day. Then around the bend, in the middle of the path, you suddenly come upon a coiled-up snake ready to strike at you. A deep chill of fear shoots through your body. Before you think a thought, your heart starts pumping rapidly, your palms sweat, and your muscles fill with the extra blood supply you need to sprint to safety. No thought goes through your mind; you become entirely part of the moment. For a split-second you freeze, then immediately see a path out, and you are ready to bolt.

But just as you're taking off, the sun comes out. Gradually, through the placid movement of clouds overhead, light replaces shadow, and blades of grass become clear and distinct. The path is there beside you again, all laid out just as before. Then it dawns on you that the snake you thought you were looking at was not a snake at all but simply an old piece of coiled-up rope. You stare, amazed and relieved at this now-altered apparition. You take a breath. Your *thinking* brain—your *prefrontal cortex*—that had shut down comes back online and tells your *feeling/sensing* brain and body—your *limbic system*—that the snake it thought it saw is not a snake after all, just an inanimate object.

You can relax, breathe again, and let go of your tension. Your body can settle down. The thinking part of your brain helps you put the whole situation into perspective and moderates your fear through observation, understanding, and insight. Your body slowly returns to normal as you tell yourself that you have nothing to be scared of. You take more deep breaths, shake your arms and legs a bit, or jog a few yards to get rid of the excess adrenaline your body just built up, and your muscles start to regain their supple, natural state.

Nature evolved this fear response so that if we sense danger or feel threatened, our feeling of fear will signal our *fight/flight/ freeze* mechanisms to go into self-defense mode. This fight/flight/ freeze response is part of our limbic system. Our limbic system operates hundreds of times faster than our thinking mind because nature does not want us to think about whether or not we should run from a saber-toothed tiger or an oncoming truck. She wants us just to run, stand and fight, or freeze in our tracks till peril, hopefully, passes us by.

The Limbic System: Our Emotional Processing Center

We process emotions like fear and love, key to our human and animal experience, through our limbic system. Scientists sometimes refer to the limbic brain/body system as the "reptilian" or "animal" brain or the "feeling/sensing" part of the brain, and the prefrontal cortex as the "thinking/reasoning brain." The limbic system developed long before the prefrontal cortex ever made its appearance on the evolutionary stage. Feelings, so necessary to our survival, came first. Thinking came thousands of years later.

The limbic system is the part of our brain and body that processes our emotions and the information picked up by our senses: what we see, hear, smell, taste, and touch. It "holds," records, and categorizes our emotional memories and the sensory data that goes along with them. We're not necessarily aware of the limbic system as it gathers, records, and indexes these sights, sounds, and smells, and the emotions we're experiencing until our thinking mind elevates these imprints to a conscious level and makes sense of them. But these emotional and sensory "files" are there nonetheless.

Mind/Body Connection

The limbic system has a huge job: it has to do something with all of the sights, sounds, tastes, smells, and touch sensations that it is constantly gathering from the world around us. And it also has to process the feelings that are attached to that sensory information. The various jobs of the limbic system are far-reaching and crucial. It governs and regulates our mood, appetite, libido, sleep cycles, motivation, and bonding, to name just a few of its wide-ranging functions. If our limbic system gets thrown out of balance, through, for example, repeated experiences of fear, abuse, or neglect, we can have difficulty regulating our basic emotions and our emotional connection with others. Lack of limbic regulation can manifest as depression, anxiety, or sleep disturbances. Limbic disregulation can also cause difficulty in regulating mood, appetite, sexual responses, bonding, and motivation. Those affected by trauma (and a disregulated limbic system) can thus have trouble living moderately. Instead, they vacillate between life's emotional extremes.

Trauma and Our Loss of Self Regulation

We all have an "emotional set point," a default setting that represents our personal "norm." It's a set point that we can continually return to as our point of emotional balance and equilibrium out of which our thinking, feeling, and behavior grows. Trauma disturbs that delicate balance. It upsets the equilibrium and can cause us to lose our ability to return easily to our emotional set point because it has been disrupted too deeply and too often. We have become overwhelmed too frequently with too much feeling and slammed our foot on the emotional brakes too often. Our emotional gearshift gets eroded. We have trouble finding neutral.

When I see people who cannot find their way back to their emotional set points or a normal range of functioning, I look for fear, stress, or relationship trauma of some kind because these extremes tend to be a direct result of the cumulative effect of trauma. We overreact or under react but we have trouble with "normal". Overreactions and underreactions send up a signal to me as a therapist that further investigation is merited. I ask myself, *Why does this person fear going near to this feeling? Why is she hiding from the feeling either by acting it out, medicating it, or shutting it down? Why is she staying away from that emotional middle ground where she can feel and think about feeling at the same time? What doesn't she want to feel and why doesn't she want to feel it?*

Experience Becomes Biology

While it's our limbic system that processes our emotions and collects and categorizes information gathered by our senses, it is our thinking brain that elevates that data to a conscious level and converts it into language or pictures that have meaning attached to them. Through this rational thinking of the prefrontal cortex, we

integrate the disparate fragments of our experience into a coherent whole—a "picture" or "story"—that we can record, remember,
and recall. It's through this rational thinking that we make sense
of ourselves and ourselves in relation to others. The limbic system
provides content. The prefrontal cortex categorizes that content,
gives it a framework, and integrates it into a working model of
ourselves and our lives.

But what happens when that thinking doesn't take place
because the prefrontal cortex was temporarily frozen with fear?
Trauma causes the prefrontal cortex to temporarily shut down
while still allowing the limbic system to keep going. This means
that we continue to record content but we are not making sense
of that content. Where do all our feelings go if the thinking brain
doesn't help us to understand them? And what about the images,
sounds, smells, tastes, and textures that are part of an experience?
Did these things happen? Did they disappear? Where are they?
Without the help of the prefrontal cortex, all of that emotional
and sensory information gets recorded by the limbic brain/body
but remains unprocessed and unconscious. Because the prefrontal cortex was not doing its job of elevating the information to a
conscious level and making sense of it, those emotions and sense
impressions were stored within us but remain unconscious. In
cases such as this, the body remembers but the mind "forgets."
The trauma-related "memories" become part of the vast web of
what researchers call a dissociated neural net or the dissociative
capsule (Badenbock 2008; Scaer 2005). The feelings and fragments of sensory experience and emotion are in us, but we don't
know just where and how they fit into the total picture.

Triggers

But out of sight is not out of mind/body. These limbic memories can be triggered without our awareness. As these memories are unconsciously triggered and replayed, their grooves deepen. Unless we make our unconscious limbic memories conscious so that we can feel, think, and talk about them, so that we can process and become aware of what is inside of us, we can become locked in a recycled memory that does not seem to have a beginning, middle, or an end and deepen its imprint in our mind/body. In his book *The Trauma Spectrum: Hidden Wounds and Human Resiliency*, Dr. Robert Scaer writes:

> *When people develop PTSD, the replaying of the trauma (in the mind) leads to [neurological] sensitization. With every replay of the trauma there is increasing distress. In those individuals, the traumatic event, which started out as a social, interpersonal process, develops secondary biological consequences that are hard to reverse once they become entrenched. Because these patients have intolerable sensations and feelings, their tendency is to avoid them. Mentally they "split off" or "dissociate these feelings," physically their bodies tighten and brace against them. They seem to live under the assumption that if they feel these sensations and feelings those feelings will overwhelm them forever. These are patients who rely on medications, drugs and alcohol to make these feelings go away because they have lost the confidence that they can tolerate them on their own . . . The fear of being consumed by these terrible feelings makes them feel that only not feeling them will make them go away (2005).*

Other common ways that people try to get rid of these unconscious, unwanted feelings are by acting them out through behaviors that are destructive to the self, other people, or relationships (picking fights, becoming passive aggressive, constant complaining, self-sabotaging behaviors), or by projecting them onto others and disowning them within the self (making them about something that someone else did or a situation or circumstance outside the self), or engaging in process addictions (over- or undereating, risky, or overly frequent sexual liaisons).

These fragmented memories that contain valuable information about our experience and ourselves become hidden from view. And until we make them conscious, parts of our inner world, parts of who we are and why we do what we do, can remain a mystery to us.

SIX

The Traumatized Self:
Falling Apart on the Inside

When you're born, a light is switched on, a light which
shines up through your life. As you get older the light
still reaches you, sparkling as it comes up through
your memories. And if you're lucky as you travel forward
through time, you'll bring the whole of yourself along with
you, gathering your skirts and leaving nothing behind,
nothing to obscure the light. But if a Bad Thing happens, part
of you is seared into place and trapped forever at that time.
The rest of you moves onward, dealing with all the todays
and tomorrows, but something, some part of you, is left behind.
That part blocks the light, colors the rest of your life,
but worse than that, it's alive. Trapped forever at that moment,
and alone in the dark, that part of you is still alive.

—Michael Marshall Smith, *Only Forward*

Situations that explode our sense of what "normal" is can leave
us feeling shaken and shattered. They can also leave us with
a fragmented sense of our inner world. Significant traumatic

moments may remain unprocessed within us due to the phenomenon of psychic numbing or the mind's urge to throw frightening circumstances out of conscious awareness at the very same time that it is recording emotions and sense impressions that are part of that very experience.

A Mind/Body Picture of PTSD

It has long been recognized that the disturbing experience of war can produce reactions of shell shock or battle fatigue causing those who experience them to suffer both personally and in relationships long after they return home. Professionals in the mental health field began to recognize that children who grew up with adverse childhood experiences exhibited many of the same post-traumatic stress disorder (PTSD) symptoms that returning Vietnam war veterans exhibited (van der Kolk 1987). Following are some of the mind/body phenomena that underlie PTSD and cause it to have long-term impact.

Problems with Self-Regulation

The loss of neuromodulation (the ability to regulate moods) that is at the core of PTSD can lead to emotional dysregulation. Traumatized people tend to go immediately from stimulus to response without being able to first figure out what makes them so upset. They tend to experience intense fear, anxiety, anger, and panic in response to even minor stimuli. This can make them either overreact and intimidate others, or shut down and freeze (van der Kolk 1994).

Dysregulation involves both the mind and the body. We move from states of hyperarousal (that may include heart pounding, sweating, increased adrenaline, shortness of breath, dry throat, or shaking) to shutting down. Our emotions run strong when traumatic moments from our past are triggered in our present; we can have racing thoughts and disruptive imagery that dance along the surface of our mind. Because we experience these emotions and sensations in our bodies and because they are actually physical, we may want to swing into some form of action. Then, if action seems futile or impossible, we shut down; we go numb. This is the trauma dance: high intensity reactions followed by shutting down. Twelve-step programs have a colloquial expression for this cycling, referring to it as "black-and-white thinking." We move from one extreme to the other and have trouble holding an intelligent center.

Hypervigilance/Anxiety

Hypervigilance is a symptom of PTSD and refers to the experience of being constantly tense and on guard. People experiencing this symptom of PTSD tend to scan their environment and relationships for signs of potential danger or repeated relationship insults and ruptures (van der Kolk 1987). At extreme levels, hypervigilance may appear similar to paranoia. The individual is constantly trying to read the faces of those in the environment in order to protect themselves against perceived pain or humiliation. Unfortunately, this hair-trigger reactivity can lead to perceptions of problems that do not exist, and, inadvertently, to their development, or to an exaggeration of problems that might have been easily managed.

Van der Kolk describes hypervigilance as an enhanced state of sensory sensitivity accompanied by an exaggerated intensity of behaviors whose purpose is to detect threats (van der Kolk 1987). Hypervigilance can also be accompanied by physical symptoms such as a state of increased anxiety, which can cause exhaustion, abnormally increased arousal, or a high responsiveness to stimuli. People experiencing hypervigilance may become preoccupied with studying their environment for possible threats, causing them to lose connections with their family and friends. They will overreact to loud and unexpected noises, become agitated in highly crowded or noisy environments, and may have a difficult time getting to sleep or staying asleep (van der Kolk 1987).

Numbing of Responsiveness/Emotional Constriction

Numbing is a natural part of the trauma response and may mean that those who have experienced trauma have a restricted range of feelings that they are comfortable experiencing and expressing.

Aware of their difficulties in controlling their emotions, traumatized people seem to spend their energies on avoiding distressing internal sensations, instead of attending to the demands of the environment. In addition, they lose satisfaction in matters that previously gave them a sense of satisfaction and may feel "dead to the world." This emotional numbing may be expressed as depres-

sion, as anhedonia and lack of motivation, as psychosomatic reactions, or as dissociative states. In contrast with the intrusive PTSD symptoms, which occur in response to outside stimuli, numbing is part of these patients' baseline functioning. In children, numbing has been observed among elementary school children attacked by a sniper, among witnesses to parental assault or murder, and among victims of physical or sexual abuse. They become less involved in playful social interactions, and often are withdrawn and isolated. After being traumatized, many people stop feeling pleasure from exploration and involvement in activities and they feel that they just "go through the motions" of everyday living. Emotional numbness also gets in the way of resolving the trauma in psychotherapy: they give up on recovery and it keeps them from being able to imagine a future for themselves (van der Kolk 1994).

Somatic Disturbances: Body Aches and Pains

When a person is unable to experience or act on powerful emotions, those emotions may be experienced somatically as back pain, chronic headaches, muscle tightness or stiffness, stomach problems, heart pounding, or headaches. People traumatized as children may suffer from alexithymia—an inability to translate somatic sensations into feelings such as anger, happiness, or fear. This failure to translate somatic states into words and symbols causes them to experience emotions simply as physical problems (Saxe et al 1994).

Learning Difficulties

Physiological hyperarousal interferes with the capacity to concentrate, attend, and learn from experience. Aside from amnesias about aspects of the trauma, traumatized people often have trouble remembering ordinary events as well. Easily triggered into hyperarousal by trauma-related stimuli, along with a compromised ability to attend and pay attention, they may display symptoms of attention deficit/hyperactivity disorder.

Unresolved grief can also contribute to learning disabilities. In a study of bereaved adults with learning disabilities, only about half were known to have attended the funeral of their deceased parent (Hollins and Sinason 2000). As a group, these bereaved adults demonstrated more psychopathology and behavioral disturbances, including irritability, anxiety, adjustment difficulties, and depression than the controls. Nearly three-quarters of them were unaware of any connection between blocking their grief and their learning issues. A follow-up of this study group after five years pointed to the likelihood of delayed and/or prolonged grief in many people with learning disabilities, particularly those who had not had a bereavement-related intervention (Bonell-Pascual et al 1999), such as a funeral. This doesn't mean that all losses require intervention, only that loss needs to be somehow felt and processed; funerals, friends, and family can be sufficient supports if not avoided. But family traumas, such as addiction, divorce, or dysfunction, often go unacknowledged and without bereavement.

Sleep Problems

Adults and children with hyperarousal and a loss of neuro-modulation may experience sleep problems, both because they are unable to still themselves sufficiently to go to sleep and because they are fearful of having traumatic nightmares. Many traumatized people report dream-interruption insomnia: they wake themselves up as soon as they start having a dream for fear that the dream will turn into a trauma-related nightmare. They are also liable to exhibit hypervigilance, an exaggerated startle response, and restlessness.

Aggression, Anger, or Rage Against Self and Others

Issues with anger and aggression are part of the PTSD syndrome; ACoAs can carry resentments that morph into problems with anger management, rage issues, acting out behaviors, passive aggression, or self-medicating. They may not even know they are angry; that anger may be quite unconscious and unprocessed.

Another manifestation of unprocessed anger is depression. ACoAs may turn their anger against themselves and become listless, isolated, and sullen. Or they may act it out; they become the screw-up and blow up their own lives. They drink, drug, cut, or fall apart, engaging full-out in self-destructive behaviors that undermine their happiness and success. All of these are ways of not feeling the anger they carry.

Numerous studies have demonstrated that both adults and children who have been traumatized are likely to turn their aggression against others or themselves. Being abused as a child sharply increases the risk for later delinquency and violent criminal behavior. In one study of 87 psychiatric outpatients we found that self-mutilators invariably had severe childhood histories of abuse and/or neglect. There is good evidence that self-mutilative behavior is related to endogenous opioid changes in the CNS secondary to early traumatization. Problems with aggression against others have been particularly well documented in war veterans, traumatized children and in prisoners with histories of early trauma (van der Kolk et al 1991).

Learned Helplessness

When we feel that nothing we can do will affect or change the situation we're in, we may develop learned helplessness. We may lose some of our ability to take actions to affect change (Peterson, Maier, and Seligman 1995). As a technical term in animal and human psychology, learned helplessness refers to a state of collapse in which one behaves helplessly, even when the opportunity is restored to help one's self by avoiding a dangerous or harmful situation.

Research studies found that the strongest predictor of a depressive response to a situation is a perceived lack of control over a circumstance. Illustrating this point are experiments done with people performing mental tasks while there is distracting noise. Those who had access to and could use a switch to turn off the noise had improved performance, even though they rarely bothered to do so. Simply knowing this option was available was enough to substantially counteract its distracting effect (Blumenthal et al 1999).

Making positive choices builds resilience and makes it less

likely that those affected by adverse circumstances will develop PTSD. Even participating in cleanup efforts of one's environment after a disaster builds resilience. Children who are trapped in dysfunctional homes benefit by making choices to better their lives in small ways; babysitting to get out of the house and earn some money and having extracurricular activities, friends, or programs to attend where they can feel safe, can all reduce the feeling of being trapped and helpless. Recovery for ACoAs is also a way of beginning a choice-making process that will counter the effects of learned helplessness.

Intrusive Reexperiencing

Traumatized people may experience past trauma intruding into their "normal" consciousness in a variety of ways—through memories, dreams, distress responses, or flashbacks. They may have flashes of traumatic imagery, overpowering emotions, or feel defined by what happened to them and fearful of a repetition of anything like it occurring again. Remembrance and intrusion of the trauma is expressed on many different levels, ranging from flashbacks; mood swings; somatic sensations, or body aches; nightmares; interpersonal reenactments, including transference repetitions; personality characteristics; and pervasive themes that play out in one's life.

Dissociation/Memory Disturbances

Extreme fear such as that experienced by CoAs can cause them to "leave their bodies," to feel they do not "live in their own skin," so to speak. There may be an experience of "derealization"—or feeling as if they or the world is not "real"—and "depersonalization"—feeling as if they are losing their identity or adopting a new identity. Dissociation can involve a feeling of disconnection from the body or surroundings, either momentary or lasting ones. Dissociation may also involve "losing time" or experiencing amnesia regarding entire traumatic events or significant periods of them.

The person who dissociates has "difficulty tolerating and regulating intense emotional experiences. This problem results in part from having had little opportunity to learn to soothe oneself or modulate feelings, due to growing up in an abusive or neglectful family, where parents did not teach these skills" (Rauch, Metcalfe, and Jacobs 1996; van der Kolk and Fisler 1996). When we feel overwhelmed with intense emotion that we cannot regulate, we psychically and emotionally disconnect from the situation that is overwhelming us while still staying physically in it. We zone out, and "depersonalization, derealization, amnesia and identity confusion can all be thought of as efforts at self-regulation when affect regulation fails. Each psychological adaptation changes the ability of the person to tolerate a particular emotion, such as feeling threatened" (ibid).

During the stage of life that children naturally try on different identities in their daily play activities, children who are exposed to prolonged and severe trauma may even be capable of organizing whole different personality fragments in order to cope with traumatic experiences. Over a long period of time, and in cases where there is severe trauma, this may give rise to the syndrome of dissociative identity disorder (DID), which may occur in about 4 percent of psychiatric inpatients in the United States (Saxe et al 1993).

Desire to Self-Medicate

Someone who is coping with the sorts of symptoms here described may become engaged in a compulsive relationship with alcohol, drugs, food, sex, work, or money as a way of quieting the disturbing mental, physiological, and emotional disequilibration that the symptoms engender. Self-medicating can seem to be a solution, a way to calm an inner storm and restore "balance," as it really does make pain, anxiety, and body symptoms temporarily abate. But in the long run, it creates many more problems than it solves.

Hyperreactivity

Living with relationship trauma can oversensitize us to stress, causing us to overrespond to stressful situations and blowing out of proportion conflicts that could be managed calmly; we overreact. This hyperreactivity can emerge whether we are in a slow grocery line, in traffic, at work, or in relationships. Triggers can be stimuli reminiscent of relationship trauma. Feeling helpless, rejected, abandoned, or humiliated can trigger old vulnerability. Being around yelling or criticism, or even observing certain facial expressions on others, may trigger a stronger reaction than is appropriate to the situation. So can being in closed-in places that make one feel trapped. Because traumatized people often have a loss of neuromodulation and self-regulation, they may not be able to "right size" their emotions once they have been triggered. They may explode and get aggressive or implode and withdraw. Working with these triggers and working through the unconscious feelings from the past that drive them is central to the treatment of the ACoA trauma syndrome.

SEVEN

Relationship Trauma: When Home Is No Longer Safe

Lunatics are similar to designated hitters. Often an
entire family is crazy, but since an entire family
can't go into the hospital, one person is designated as crazy
and goes inside. Then, depending on how the rest of the family
is feeling, that person is kept inside or snatched out, to prove
something about the family's mental health.

—Susanna Kaysen, *Girl, Interrupted*

Relationship trauma constitutes the cumulative and long-term effect of traumatic relational moments or relational dynamics on the brain and body. Virtually all the trauma I deal with occurs within the context of primary attachment relationships. Traumatic relational moments are a part of anyone's life; they are not necessarily out of the norm but they can become more frequent and more intense in families that struggle with addiction and the cluster of abusive behaviors that often surround addiction. "While most studies on PTSD have been done on adults, particularly on war veterans, in recent years, a small prospective literature has emerged which calls attention to the differential effects of trauma at various age levels. Anxiety disorders, chronic hyperarousal, and reenactments have now been described with some regularity in acutely traumatized children" (van der Kolk and Saporta 1991). "In addition to the reactions to discrete, one-time, traumatic incidents documented in these studies, intrafamilial abuse must certainly be included among the most severe traumas encountered by human beings" (ibid).

Relationship ruptures are experienced as traumatic because we are neurologically wired for powerful relationship attachments; "neurons are genetically primed to support connections through the relational experiences we have with those closest to us. The patterns of energy and information laid down in these early moments of meeting develop the actual structure of these limbic regions" (Badenoch 2008). We wire co-states or relationship dynamics into our very self and then we look to re-create both sides of those dynamics as we engage in relationships throughout our lives. The dynamics we experience as children template what we look for, expect, and re-create in adult relationships. "The biological effects of developmental trauma have best been studied in young nonhuman primates, who in many ways resemble young human beings. Forty years of primate research has firmly established that early disruption of the social attachment bond reduces the long-term capacity to cope with subsequent social disruptions and to modulate physiological arousal" (van der Kolk and Saporta 1991). In other words, when we have been traumatized in childhood within our primary relationships, we have trouble modulating the intense feelings that adult intimacy brings up.

Growing children are practicing at mediating and managing overwhelming feeling states. They are learning how to restore balance and calm after feeling overwhelmed; they learn by modeling someone who can show them how to do that and being actively helped to learn how to restore balance. This builds resilience. But when this help is unavailable and when family chaos is causing the stress, the child is left to manage on his own. In a traumatic moment, the central nervous system (CNS) is simultaneously revved for fight and flight and flooded with body chemicals to inhibit fight or flight unless absolutely necessary. The firing of the CNS in opposing directions causes the child to freeze. The longer he spends in this state, the more likely he is to feel trapped and helpless and have no way of learning to manage his overwhelming emotions. Rather than learning lessons of resilience, his body is pounded with ever-increasing levels of stress. The child is not able to fully process the overwhelming emotions and impressions that are part of these traumatic moments so the fear he experiences as well as key fragments of experience and information may get split off or dissociated from. And because of a child's limited intellectual development, he is unable to make mature sense of what's going on. Children often imagine that they have somehow created the frightening situation and that it is somehow their job to correct it. They imagine that there is probably something wrong with them.

The Unique Dilemma of the CoA and the ACoA

Children love their parents and want to rely on them, and they do relay on them no matter who those parents are. But addiction plays havoc with family dynamics. For example, spouses of alcoholics can become less available to their children and can build up years of resentment toward the position their alcoholic partner has put them in. Spouses often get stuck "keeping the show on the road," so to speak, as their alcoholic/addicted partner falls in and out of sobriety. The sober parent becomes the reliable one. And as they are repeatedly put in this role, they may even lose their own spontaneity and ease. Their resentment builds, and the more it builds, the more unavailable they become to the child and, for that matter, to themselves. Then the child is robbed of easy relating with two parents. In this scenario, the alcoholic may even emerge as the fun and available parent. After all, they aren't always drunk or high. Sometimes they are sober, or relaxed from a couple of drinks, or in a generous, expansive mood. The reliable parent, the one who takes the child to the dentist and buys new shoes, may powerfully resent it when it is obvious that the child prefers the fun parent.

What a confusing mess to untangle. So confusing that ACoAs often don't want to go near to it. This primary but disorganized attachment with an alcoholic parent (and perhaps the other parent) can present problems for ACoAs later in life. They cling to their happy moments with all their strength because the very same person who cut them to the quick may have been the one they went to in order to feel reassured and good about themselves.

The human response to trauma is so constant across traumatic stimuli that it is safe to say that the central nervous system (CNS) seems to react to any overwhelming, threatening and uncontrollable experience in quite a consistent pattern. Regardless of these circumstances, traumatized people are prone to have intrusive memories of elements of the trauma, to have a poor tolerance for arousal, to respond to stress in an all-or-nothing way, and to feel emotionally numb. All of these psychological phenomena must have a basis in biological functioning, some of these relationships between biological states are now ready to be explored. PTSD as defined in the DSM-III-R highlights those post-traumatic symptoms that are most clearly biologically based (for reviews see van der Kolk, 1987; Krystal et al., 1989); the secondary post-traumatic changes in identity and interpersonal relations are slated to be classified in the separate category of Disorders of Extreme Stress Not Otherwise Specified (DESNOS) in the DSM-IV (van der Kolk and Saporta 1991).

The fact that the emphasis in the psychiatric manual that defines PTSD is on biological rather than relational effects of trauma means that those who have been traumatized in relationships fall randomly into and all over the healthcare, legal, and penal system, and receive a variety of "diagnoses" that do not speak to the trauma that may have engendered their symptoms. Healing actually needs to be about adopting a new design for living as well as receiving therapy aimed at resolving the unconscious effects of trauma to the mind, emotions, and body.

Why Traumatic Moments Get "Sticky"

When the people we have a profound need to stay close to are the ones hurting us, our experience of those traumatic moments and relationship dynamics can become very "sticky," holding us like psychological glue to old, rigid, and reactive patterns of relating that do not easily change. Here's why: our previous experiences set us up for how we see ourselves and how we live our lives. They prime us for what to expect from others, from life, and from relationships. Daniel Siegel, author of *Mindsight: The New Science of Personal Transformation*, explains: "Prior learning sends related information down from the top layers of our six-neuron-deep column to shape our perception of what we are seeing or hearing or touching or smelling or tasting . . . perception is virtually always a blend of what we are sensing now and what we've learned previously" (2010). Because sense impressions get overlapped with emotions, and in the case of relationship trauma, those emotions may be fraught with fear and anxiety; we may defend against feeling or "remembering" them. Thus we feel closed, defensive, and unwilling to change.

Dr. Siegel describes the neural process of "stuckness" and "openness" as states of mind:

> Sometimes the adhesive holding a state [of mind] is flexible, enabling us to be receptive and open to bringing in new sensory data and new ways of behaving . . . but sometimes engrained states are more "sticky" and restrictive, locking us into old patterns of neural firing, tying us to previously learned information, priming us to react in rigid ways. This locked-down state is "reactive"—meaning that our behavior, in large part, is determined by a prior learning and is often survival-based and automatic. We react reflexively rather than responding openly . . . primed by old learning (2010).

In other words, we get stuck repeating and re-creating varieties of thinking, feeling, and behavior from the past that overtake the present moment. We worry that if we enter the "we" state, we will get slammed. We need to learn that a "we state" is safe in order to enter it, or we need to be able to examine why it isn't, so that we can learn a new way of being with others while sustaining ourselves, so that a "we state" starts to feel manageable. All of this becomes part of a therapeutic process, part of recovery from trauma.

Trauma-Engendering Family Dynamics

Just as a person can get stuck in living in extremes, so can an entire family. The pattern of alternating between *imploding* and *exploding*, or cycling between states of *high intensity* then *numbing* or *shutting down*, or the opposite of going from a *numb, imploded state* toward *explosiveness*, can become part of a disregulated emotional and behavioral pattern that is common to addicted and/or trauma-engendering families. These families can be steeped in patterns that may have been building over a period of years. For these reasons, they may have trouble seeing themselves clearly or seeking help or having the leftover energy or motivation to make positive changes. They are focused on survival, and the more they "survive," the more "glued" they become to their survival mode.

Impulsivity versus Rigidity/Control

When family members have a hard time tolerating or "holding" intense states of emotion, those emotions may surface and be acted out through impulsive behaviors that engender chaos. Painful feelings that are too hard to sit with explode into the container of the family and get acted out rather than talked out. Blame; anger; rage; emotional, physical, or sexual abuse; collapsing into helplessness; withdrawal or yelling; over- or underspending; and sexual acting out are some ways of acting out emotional and psychological pain in dysfunctional ways that engender chaos.

When the family starts to feel like things are getting out of control, members see the solution to that as clamping down hard to restore order and reduce chaos. They get *rigid and controlling*. Parents may tighten up on rules and routines in an attempt to ward off the feeling of falling apart. Or family members may become both controlled and controlling in their behavior in an attempt to manage inner feelings of chaos. Thus the dynamic of cycling back and forth between impulsive or chaotic behavior and rigid control takes hold. There is a lack of middle ground where strong feelings can be talked over or even explode momentarily but then be worked through toward some sort of tolerable resolution. Again, there is the tendency to alternate black-and-white thinking, feeling, and behavior, with no shades of gray—another reflection of the family's problems with regulation.

Enmeshment/Disengagement/Avoidance

Over closeness that doesn't really allow for much breathing room and natural space in relationships is called enmeshment.

Huddling together to form "special" bonds, seeing eye to eye, triangulating (two family members talking about a third but never addressing the issue directly with that third person), or allying together against the powers that be can help scared family members feel less alone and crazy. Siblings may form covert bonds or a parent may turn a child into a surrogate partner and confidante to compensate for the absence of intimacy with the partner. But this sort of enmeshed closeness does not really allow much breathing room, and it can split the family into factions. The loyalty it demands can also preclude honest, comfortable relating.

Enmeshment is a relational style that lacks boundaries and often discourages differences or disagreement, seeing them not as healthy and natural but as disloyal or even threatening. Enmeshed styles of relating formed in childhood tend to repeat themselves in adult relationships.

The other side of enmeshment is disengagement. Many addicted families cycle back and forth between enmeshment and disengagement; they yearn for closeness but lack the kinds of healthy boundaries that would let them take space, hold different points of view, or hang onto a sense of self while in each other's presence. Consequently, enmeshed forms of closeness becomes suffocating. Then family members see disengaging through withdrawing, fighting, or avoiding each other as the only way of getting some personal space. They see the solution for feeling overwhelmed with too much closeness as doing the direct opposite: they disengage. Or they avoid subjects, people, places, and things that might trigger discomfort or disagreement, which also can lead to emotional disengagement.

Overfunctioning versus Underfunctioning

When people don't play their position in a volleyball game, the ball drops. The same thing can be true in the alcoholic family system. Balls are dropping all over the place. Who is going to pick them up? In an attempt to maintain family balance, some members may swoop in and play more than their own role; they overfunction in order to compensate for the underfunctioning of others.

Overfunctioning can wear many hats; children may become little parents and overfunction by taking care of younger siblings when parents do not fulfill their normal duties. CoAs may take care of parents emotionally, becoming little partners. Or they may work overtime striving to restore order and dignity to a family who is rapidly slipping. Spouses may overfunction to maintain order while the addict falls in and out of normal functioning.

The learned helplessness that is part of the trauma response, in which one comes to feel that nothing they can do will make a difference or make things better so they give up, can lead to underfunctioning. Family members may find themselves unable to mobilize, get their lives together, and make useful choices.

It is also not uncommon that the addict or the spouse may do both, overfunctioning to make up for periods of underfunctioning. Again we see yet another version of a lack of ability to self-regulate or for the family system to work as a team where each member is expected to carry their load, to suit up and show up.

Caretaking versus Neglect

When monkeys grieve, they step up their grooming and caretaking behaviors. Suddenly their partner's coats are full of nits that need attending to or their children need extra rocking. Sometimes, we take care of something in others because ·we yearn for some sense of closeness and connection; we try to give to another person what feels missing for us. We project our own unconscious anxiety or pain onto someone else, seeing it as about them rather than understanding it as our own. Then we set about fixing them instead of ourselves. It is a form of caretaking that is all too often motivated by our own unidentified pain rather than a genuine awareness of another's. Because this is the case, neglect can be its dark side. We neglect or don't see real need within another person because we can't identify real need within ourselves. Not surprisingly, our care of the other person is not always appreciated by them, nor does it necessarily feel all that good to them. In fact, it can even ask them to become needy in the same area that we're needy. This can actually have the effect of distancing them because our "care" feels cloying and unattuned.

Withholding attention or simply ignoring or not seeing another's need are forms of neglect and can hurt people deeply; we are wired for clan and connection, and shunning can feel like punishment. People who suffer from feeling neglected can be hard to treat as there is no obvious abuse to point a finger at. They often report feeling that they have too many needs for anyone to meet, and they can be mistrustful of deep connection. Consequently, they may push away the very thing—relationship—that might help them to heal.

When we feel emotionally wounded, we may react by going to one of two extremes. We may anxiously cling to others through caretaking, or we may push closeness away by neglect-ful, abandoning behaviors . . . or we may alternate between the two. We get over close through unattuned caretaking or under close through neglect—both effective means of warding off our fears of our own neediness and emotional pain.

Low Self-Worth versus Grandiosity

Feelings of low self-worth and shame can be engendered by living with the discouraging and sad spectrum of addiction and trauma. Not feeling normal, feeling different from other families, and hiding the painful truth of family dysfunction can all con-tribute to those in an addicted family system feeling bad about themselves. When all of our best attempts to make a situation better add up to naught, we may start to wonder what is wrong with other people, with life, and with us.

A common defense against feelings of worthlessness is gran-diosity. Feelings of helplessness, frustration, and inadequacy get covered up with grandiose schemes and fantasies. Family mem-bers may not understand how to take baby steps toward success or getting their lives together. Frustrated and disheartened, they may take refuge in grandiose ideas about themselves as a way of warding off ever-growing fears that their lives are somewhat unmanageable or they cannot seem to get things to work out for them. We all know the big talker, or conversely the quiet, privately superior person who, to cover up feelings of worthless-ness that they cannot admit to, feels in some way superior as a defense against feeling inferior.

Abuser versus Victim

Where the power balance is fairly even between family members, the roles of abuser and victim can be traded back and forth many times within the same interaction. Sometimes the roles become stratified and certain family members become the obvious abusers while others become the obvious victims. Entitled abusers who somehow feel they have the right to aggressively subjugate others damage the self-esteem of those around them. Living with them is destructive both emotionally and psychologically. Victims are those who may be being abused through no fault of their own; they are at the short end of a power dynamic either because of size, place in the family, or a power imbalance of some sort in the system. Certainly small children are sitting ducks for being abused and victimized by out-of-control parents and older siblings. But one thing is for sure: both roles are present in dysfunctional or addicted family systems. And both roles can become relationship dynamics that get carried along through life.

Unfortunately, the abused child, the *victim*, is at risk, without recovery, of becoming an abusing parent, of passing on their pain to the next generation. The victim role can become dysfunctional and can be used as a convoluted and passive way of getting power. Entitled victims are also tough to live with—they may subjugate others through passive aggression by "falling apart" or "collapsing" as a way of getting someone else to rescue them; they learn that crisis gets them the attention that they long for. They can feel very entitled to nurse their grudges and demand more than their share of care and attention. And because they feel like they are victims, they do not want to see ways in which they may be victimizing others and flipping the role of the abused into the abuser.

Denial versus Despair

Families don't fall apart all at once; they do it in excruciating detail. Bit by tiny bit, the seams start to split, the dam breaks, and bit by bit, they come up with excuses to cover up their ever-increasing anxiety—that what they fear may be happening is, in fact, happening. Denial is a dysfunctional attempt to ward off feelings of fear, anxiety, and despair. "My husband loves his 'relaxation time' before dinner; he just wants to be home with his family" (Read: where he can drink in peace); "My wife has the flu again" (Read: is drunk); "Our family is spontaneous—we don't like to making rigid plans" (Read: we have learned that making plans is disappointing and futile as they often fall apart at the zero hour.) But eventually they can't tell a lie from the truth. They become confused about what they feel and doubt their own best thinking.

As despair and anxious preoccupation grow, so does the need for more complex forms of denial. And as denial takes the place of honest and measured self-disclosure, worries and anxieties remain hidden and unaddressed. Family members become increasingly preoccupied with managing their ever-increasing unmanageability and despairing of ever being happy again. And the more despairing they become, the greater their need to actively deny. Little by little, one situation at a time, reality gets rewritten as family members attempt to bend and adjust it, to make it less threatening. After all, what ordinary spouse or child wants to really know that the people they love are falling apart?

The seesawing, confusing, conflicting dynamics that we have described can leave CoAs feeling lost and rudderless. As a result, CoAs may also develop the sorts of characteristics of relationship trauma that create problems for them later in life. Or CoAs may grab onto any form of warmth or acceptance that they can come up with. If this happens, dysfunctional patterns of relating and/or self-medicating can take hold in childhood and be lived out for decades to come.

Giving a child who is faced with these less-than-optimal choices a bit of help at the right time is worth its weight in gold. The smallest thing can save a child's sanity. Faith-based institutions have a huge role to play in providing a safe haven; school programs (school itself), a grandparent, relative, or neighbor's house where the child feels safe and comfortable can make all the difference in a CoA's life. One does not need to create some powerful therapeutic intervention in the life of a CoA in order to make a big difference. An open door, a couch to curl up on, an after-school snack, or a place to play can make the essential difference for CoAs: they just need a place to go that isn't in a state of chaos, somewhere where they feel they can relax.

EIGHT

Haunted: The Symptoms of Relationship Trauma

All children wake up in a world that is not of their own mak-
ing, but children of alcoholics and other drug-addicted parents
wake up in a world that doesn't take care of them. No matter
what we name their risk factors, they still have to make their
own breakfast and find their own way.

—Jeannette Johnson, PhD

ACoAs can feel haunted by a past that they cannot wrap their
minds around. They feel confused.

John is a client in recovery from sex addiction. He came
home from school every day to a mother who was depressed
and locked in her room with booze, cigarettes, and prescription
meds, a mother who couldn't help him to manage successfully
in school and feel supported at home; she was a mother who
did just the opposite. "But she wasn't a real alcoholic," John says.
"She would get depressed and then just drink enough to feel

better." In role-playing himself as a child, he said, "But I loved my mother. I know there must have been good things. I don't want to hate her. I only wanted her to open the door to her room and come out and talk to me."

John continued his role-play speaking to his mother. "I need you. I need you to be with me. I hate school; I don't have any friends; the guys all pick on me. I need you to help me when I come home; the day is so long. I wanted to be home, outside playing. I missed you."

This combination of prescription medication, liquor, and cigarettes was what occurred "every four weeks" according to John. "I would know it. I could sense it. I would come home from school and it was like this dark cloud was hanging over the house. And she would be in her room. And I just couldn't screw up the courage to knock on that door; I guess I didn't want to see what was behind it, it scared me to see her like that."

This psychodrama I did with John shows clearly how, in a child's mind, the parent is just the parent. Children just do not understand that drugs and alcohol might be driving their parent's peculiar behavior. Even when playing the role of his mother, John resisted the idea that she was an alcoholic. In his child mind, she just was depressed and didn't want to be with him. And it was somehow his fault; he was just not worth attention.

I kept John in role reversal, playing his mother so that by "showing" us what his mother actually looked like and by my questioning him in role, he might come to better accept his mother's obvious addiction. John, as his mother, sat on the edge of the bed, head hanging down, knees splayed, with a cigarette and a cup of coffee.

John was a lonely little boy who needed his mommy to talk to about his day. When he came home from school, he would stare at a shut door that he could not screw up the courage to knock on. Eventually he would give up and slowly begin his afternoon process of getting his own snack, playing his own games, and going into the basement and making his forts to sit in. And wait. For something. For someone. He spent endless hours by himself in what he now sees as a dissociated state. He was nowhere really, suspended, lost in space. He tried to hold on. "I'll wait for Dad to come home," he would say. "And he'll take me to the diner for a hamburger. But he's so mad at Mom and I want to help her, to help her feel better. And I need him, but why doesn't he help her? And I need her, but she isn't there."

This is the kind of confusion that the child of an alcoholic/addict (CoA) carries: loving and feeling close to the same parent who is leaving him to manage all by himself. John found his solution with an older boy who took an interest in him. Carlos became his friend. They kept fish together in the basement. Carlos was John's only friend. He was all that stood between John and his deep longing and loneliness. So when Carlos told John to take his pants down and let Carlos play with him, John couldn't say no. He felt too scared. But he didn't like it. It made him shiver inside both with stimulation and fear, and the whole thing make him feel bad. But Carlos was showing more interest in him than his parents were. He longed to tell his mother. But she was behind that door.

This is often the dilemma of adult children of an alcoholic/addict (ACoAs). They long to love their parent, but their parent has transgressed so seriously that the love they long to feel is burdened with ghosts, haunting recollections, unresolved pain and resentment, and a feeling of loss. They feel guilty for their anger and resentment but are unable not to feel it. They feel sad for their parents because they know their parents struggled.

CoAs would do anything to bring a smile to the face they love, even sacrifice themselves. They feel angry because their parent doesn't see them, or neglects or abuses them. The little CoAs carry all sorts of feelings that they don't know what do with.

When these COAs grow into ACoAs and arrive at my office, they are often stuck in a state of emotional and psychological frozenness. They need to move through the feelings they never felt and complete actions that they had to hold onto because there was no safe way to cry, kick, scream, and say all that they longed to say but didn't dare. And not just their angry, hurt, and guilty feelings, but their thwarted feelings of love as well; "I love you, it hurt me to see you suffer, to want to help, and to be able to do nothing to make you happy. I tried but it didn't work, or I wound up feeling used, which made me feel like I failed you somehow—but didn't you fail me?"

Perhaps no one really has a carefree childhood, but ACoAs carry especially heavy burdens. They have all too often been traumatized by the experience of living with the abuse, neglect, and dysfunction that surrounds addiction. John found a solution with his friend Carlos, who was preoccupied with sex and initiated John into a world of "special knowledge" that made him feel powerful and less stupid and alone. This became

John's solution in life. He knew that he could feel powerful around women with whom he was sexual. As a grown man with two children and married to a woman he truly loved, John conducted the same secret life that he did as a boy. He was a devoted husband and father, but he had a side life that grew into sex addiction. He felt the same sense of power and the same sense of shame. His trigger was being ignored by his wife, who also suffered from depression; when she withdrew into her depression, he became that desperate, hurt, angry little boy again, and he acted out. Eventually the marriage fell apart and John sought treatment. What began as an innocent child's attempt to stave off loneliness because he was living with parental alcohol, prescription pills, and cigarette addiction was passed along through the generations as a process addiction that caused another generation of havoc and hurt.

Trauma can take many strange paths. With John, childhood trauma led to a sex (process) addiction. Living with neglect was traumatizing for him. He went through his childhood feeling lost and confused and likely somewhat disregulated in his limbic world. As the limbic system governs libido and bonding, John's disregulated limbic system may have contributed to his becoming hypersexual and seeking to meet his needs for intimacy by using sex to soothe himself and self-medicate his emotional pain. Limbic disregulation can as easily lead to an inability to organize one's self into meaningful work, workaholism, over- or undereating, or to over- or underspending.

The effects of being traumatized in childhood don't tend to disappear on their own; they tend to reemerge later in some form of overreaction, compulsive behavior, learning difficulty, intimacy issues, addictions, or process addictions. In this manner, pain from one generation gets passed along into the next. And no one knows quite how it happened. It seems as if each problem stands whole and on its own, but a closer examination reveals otherwise. John's story is utterly predictable. But it didn't have to be that way. Today he is a different person. But help came too late to save John and the family he loved from deep pain. So often this is the case—we wait for life to blow up before we address what needs addressing.

Today there is help all around—articles abound on these subjects, 12-step rooms are around the corner, and help is down the hall in many schools and workplaces. But we have to reach out and take hold of the help. And we have to stick with it until we can create meaningful change in our lives.

I see so many ACoAs who hurt inside but aren't able to seek out healing because the very vehicle that would help them is the one that hurt them—namely, relationships, which makes entering a therapeutic relationship seem frightening. However, blended in with their trauma-related mistrust of people can be a powerful wish to trust and depend on someone, a need that went partially unmet in their childhood. If they are willing to trust themselves and their own gut and intuition and take a leap of faith, they can heal.

Many ACoAs fear the feelings of vulnerability, sadness, and confusion that addressing their pain might bring up, and they want a quick fix. They e-mail me and wonder if I have a book to recommend, or they go to a one-week program, want to have a few appointments, and then be done with it. They want to *think* their way better, but they shy away from the deep developmental work that they need to do to heal. Their childhood trauma experience has left them feeling somewhat fragmented inside, and they fear falling apart if they let themselves enter too deeply into their early pain. For this reason, a strong network of support is an important part of recovery.

Trauma-related Characteristics

Following is a list of characteristics associated with trauma-related issues that I have complied and work with clinically.

Unresolved Grief

Grief is a process that takes time and includes many different phases and feelings. Stages of mourning that apply to loss of a loved one through death can also apply to the loss of a loved one through relationship rupture. Living with addiction can lead to painful relationship dynamics within the family that feel rupturing, such as the loss of family members to addiction; the loss of family rhythms and rituals; the loss of a comfortable and reliable family unit to grow up in; or the anxiety of wondering if parents are in the position to parent themselves and meeting their changing needs. Stages of loss, according to British psychoanalyst Jonathon Bowlby, are numbness, yearning and searching, disorganization, anger, despair, and reorganization (1969). Others who have experienced loss through parental divorce, parental incarceration, or being removed from the home and put into foster care are also likely to suffer a profound sense of grief. Thus ACoAs often need to mourn not only what happened in their childhoods, but also what never had a chance to happen.

Depression with Feelings of Despair

Research in animals and in people shows that stress or trauma early in life can sensitize the neurons and receptors throughout the central nervous system so that they become "kindled" or oversensitized; *kindling* is the biochemical process where nerve cells that help regulate emotions are overfired repeatedly by trauma's effects and thus we perpetually overrespond to stress of all kinds (van der Kolk 1987). Because the limbic system regulates mood, disregulation can lead to difficulty with managing emotional states throughout life, which may contribute to depression. Depression, in my experience, grows when we cannot express pain and anger; it relates to the emotional constriction or frozenness that is part of unresolved grief. The lack of sharing genuine feeling in the addicted home can also lead to isolation, a common feature of depression.

Avoidance/Tendency to Isolate

People who have been traumatized may avoid feelings that threaten them. Because they fear re-experiencing feelings of hopelessness, helplessness, rejection, or rage, they feel safer avoiding the kinds of honest exchanges that might be part of intimacy with themselves and others. They reason that by avoiding honest and authentic connection they will avoid being hurt, and so they isolate or significantly limit direct honesty. They avoid parts of themselves and parts of relational closeness (van der Kolk, McFarlane, and Weisauth 1996). Unfortunately social connectedness, though natural to our species, still needs to be learned and practiced. The more we isolate, the more out of practice we become at making connections with people, which can further isolate us. Support groups like 12-step programs are a godsend for those who fear direct connection as they do not require a formal "joining" and do not insist that people play a particular role. You are as welcome in the rooms as any other person in them and can participate at whatever level you choose.

Shame

Shame is a natural response to feeling that one is somehow in the wrong. Darwin observed it as a part of all cultures, both primitive and advanced, and one can identify it even in animals. For the person growing up in an addicted environment, shame becomes not so much a feeling that is experienced in relation to an incident or a situation—as is the case with guilt—but rather a basic attitude toward and about the self: "I am bad" as opposed to "I did something bad" (Bradshaw 2005). Shame can also be a condition imposed culturally from without or by living in a family that does not accept who you are as an individual or is ashamed of itself within the larger community. Shame can be experienced as a lack of energy for life, an inability to accept love and caring on a consistent basis, or as a hesitancy to move into self-affirming roles. It may play out as impulsive decision-making or an inability to make decisions at all (T. Dayton 2007).

Loss of Trust and Faith

When our personal world and the relationships within it become very unpredictable or unreliable, we may experience a loss of trust and faith (van der Kolk 1985) in both relationships and in life's ability to repair and renew itself. This is why the restoration of hope is so important in recovery (Yalom 1980). It is also underscores why having a spiritual belief system, such as that in 12-step programs or faith-based affiliations, can be so helpful in personal healing and in restoring a sense of belonging to a community where one can easily access support and friendship. Having a spiritual belief system can play an important role in personal healing by providing both hope and a sense of security despite any ongoing familial and intrapsychic chaos. It can also help the person in pain to reframe suffering and give it positive meaning, which develops resilience. A spiritual belief system can put pain in perspective and give it meaning and purpose (T. Dayton 2007).

Distorted Reasoning

Watching someone we love slowly become someone we cannot make sense of can shake us to the core. It can be disturbing, humiliating, and frightening. Family members may twist or distort their own reasoning in order to make this destabilizing experience easier to manage or less "real." Distorted reasoning can become intergenerational as children absorb, model, and live out their parent's way of thinking about and handling distressing situations, and it can affect the health of relationships. Denial of someone's behavior—for example, a distortion of the truth—is excessive minimization or rationalization. When we attempt to make distorted behavior seem somehow normal, we have to twist our own thinking to do so. Also, as children we make sense of situations with the developmental equipment we have at any given age; when we're young, we either borrow the reasoning of the adults around us or make our own childlike meaning.

Survivor's Guilt

The ACoA who "gets out" of an unhealthy family system while others remain mired within it may experience what is referred to as "survivor's guilt" (T. Dayton 2000; Lifton 1986). This is a condition wherein a person may see himself as having done something wrong by thriving when others were less able to. Survivor's guilt can lead to self-sabotage or becoming overly preoccupied with fixing one's family. ACoAs may seesaw between wanting to cut off their family—because being close makes them feel that they are sliding "backward"—and wishing to reconnect with their family so they do not have to tolerate their painful feelings of separateness and guilt. Over time, ACoAs need to learn what children who grew up in healthy families learned: how to be separate and stay connected in ways that allow them to maintain an autonomous sense of self.

Complicating survival guilt can be families who are still "in their disease" and who may feel threatened by those who are blowing the whistle. These family members may collude in blaming the whistle-blower, seeing that person as problematic or disloyal and even marginalizing or rejecting him or her. In this case, the ACoA benefits from creating strong bonds with other family systems, friends, and 12-step or healing communities.

Conflated Inner Imagery/Fused Feelings/ Behavior and Boundary Issues

Traumatic imagery and the feelings associated with them become conflated in our inner minds. Layer upon layer of experience and emotion from a variety of incidents and sources fuse together and become a well of stored, trauma-related experience that can get triggered when we are in range of something that is reminiscent of what hurt us or a relational cue that stimulates those memories. This type of conflated inner material can become sticky, leaky, and hard to "hold." Our inner boundaries around it can therefore become shaky and tenuous. Fused and conflated imagery and feelings can contribute to the emotional enmeshment that is so common with codependency when we have a hard time distinguishing our inner world from someone else's (van der Kolk 1987).

Feelings and imagery can get fused together along with behaviors in the mind/body when the emotional heat of trauma has helped to sear them together. For example, closeness can get fused with compliance, caring with control, love with fear, or sex with submission or rage.

Inability to Receive Caring and Support from Others

The numbing and the emotional constriction that are a natural part of the trauma response may influence our ability to take in care and support from others. Taking and giving support requires a level of trust and safety within the family system that trauma erodes. Also, fear sets in. We reason "What if I let support feel good? Then it will hurt all the more if and when it disappears again." So we push it away. And in dysfunctional families support can feel out of sync, because it is based on another person's needs rather than our own.

High-Risk Behaviors. Adrenaline is highly addictive to the brain and may act as a powerful mood enhancer. Speeding, sexual acting out, spending, fighting, drugging, working too hard, or other behaviors done in a way that put one at risk are some examples of high-risk behavior. Also, trauma can engender a flattened, emotional world. High-risk behaviors can be seen as an attempt to jump-start a numbed inner world by overstimulating the nervous system and body through excitation (van der Kolk 1987, T. Dayton 2007).

Traumatic Bonding

As the family members' fear increases, so does their need for protective bonds, because as the victim's dependency grows through abuse, so does his or her need for perceived protection. The intensity and quality of connectedness in families that contain repeated painful interactive patterns can create the types of bonds that people tend to form during times of crisis, referred to as traumatic bonds (Carnes 1997).

Alliances in dysfunctional families may become very critical to one's sense of self and even to one's survival. One parent may co-opt a child and form a bond against the other parent. Additionally, children who are feeling hurt and needy and who lose access to their parents as a source of reliable support may turn to each other to fill in the missing sense of security. This can develop into a traumatic sort of bond among siblings. Traumatic bonds formed in childhood tend to repeat their quality and content over and over again throughout life (T. Dayton 2007).

One can feel subjected by another person in a trauma bond and lose his sense of autonomy and personal choice. The nature of the victim/aggressor relationship can mean that one person consistently bends to the will of another and feels that he must simply go along with what the more aggressive, powerful, or older person expects of him. In this kind of bond, saying no can feel impossible, and setting boundaries can feel somewhat unthinkable. There can also be a feeling that one has to be loyal and protective of the abuser or the "other" no matter what, secrets must be kept, and if there is abuse, it cannot be talked about.

Rigid Psychological Defenses

People who are consistently wounded emotionally and are not able to openly and honestly address or process what's hurting them may develop rigid psychological defenses to manage or ward off pain. Examples of such defenses include:

- dissociation (remaining physically present but inwardly absent)

- denial (rewriting reality to be more palatable)
- splitting (seeing life and people as alternately all good or all bad)
- repression (pushing feelings down out of consciousness)
- minimization (minimizing the impact of situations or behavior)
- intellectualization (using thinking to rationalize and analyze in order to avoid feeling)
- projection (disowning one's own pain by projecting it outwardly)
- transference (transferring old pain into new relationships)
- reenactment patterns (continually re-creating dysfunctional patterns of relating whether or not they prove successful or healthy)

Repetition Compulsion/Cycles of Reenactment

Repetition compulsion is a psychological phenomenon in which we repeat the emotional, psychological, or behavioral aspects of a traumatic event over and over again without awareness, re-creating pain from yesterday in relationships and circumstances of today (Freud 1922). Partnering and parenting are particularly common ways of passing on this type of pain, as those relationships so closely mirror the family dynamics in which we may have modeled behaviors. Cycles of reenactment can take the form of repeatedly re-creating or reenacting the painful, warded off, or feared contents of the traumatic relationship dynamics, or putting oneself in situations where the dysfunctional dynamics or similar events are likely to happen again. For example, a man whose mother was an alcoholic may continually project onto his wife the disappointment and mistrust that he "warded off" experiencing toward his mother, being suspicious of her and expecting her to disappoint him.

The characteristics of relationship trauma we have discussed in the last chapters are those that CoAs learn by modeling family behavior and internalizing as their own. When they become ACoAs, these characteristics influence how they create and settle into their own adult lives and relationships. Luckily this story is not one-sided, as ACoAs also learn powerful skills of resilience and can be very ingenious and purposeful people as a way of mending and making sense of their past. Breaking out the kinds of characteristics that may have negative impact will helpfully help ACoAs become aware of potential pitfalls of growing up with addiction and/or family abuse and avoid playing them out blindly. "Awareness is prevention" (A. Dayton 2012).

The Codependency Connection: Neurobiological and Trauma-Related Factors that Contribute to Codependency

Codependency can be seen as the predictable set of qualities directly arising from how the brain/body processes fear and trauma.

Children's powerful need to attach is a primary piece of the codependency puzzle. Attachment is key to our survival, and we need it for our sense of well-being, so pathologizing attachment behaviors can be a slippery slope. But attachments that become traumatized can give rise to what we often call codependent tendencies. Codependent behaviors are more or less natural and attuned behaviors that have been stretched out of shape. The following neurological findings create a picture of the forces that may drive codependent behavior.

Fear-based relating. The prefrontal cortex is where we make decisions and long-range plans; it is where we form the mental templates that predict the future, tell us what to expect next, or how to lay out a task. It is also where we predict the behavior of those around us. When we freeze in fear, our ability to make these sorts of mental projections and leaps is affected. Trauma can cause us to overread or underread social or relational signals and lose our relational footing.

We look at other people's expressions to come up with ideas on what to think, feel, and do. Our frozen thinking combined with our hypervigilant or heightened ability to scan the environment can affect our ability to make clear and autonomous decisions.

Sense of Self. It is a gift of the prefrontal cortex that we can do something as abstract as imagine a sense of self. Our sense of self is under constant construction. We are always editing and adapting our self-concept—our "self-picture." For CoAs who are regularly in a mild to intense state of fear, the shutting down of this picturing and organizing aspect of the brain can significantly impact their ability to sustain their own concept of "self" and "self in relation"; thinking may feel frozen or confused, and emotions may feel enmeshed and indistinct.

Individuation can be tough for those who lack a clear sense of self. They may feel that if they pull away from their attachment figures they will disappear or will not have enough "self" to sustain them. Or they may fear that if they don't placate and "take care of" other people, no one will like them.

Hypervigilance. Because of the way the brain processes trauma, cumulative trauma can make us hypervigilant (van der Kolk 1987); we become hyperresponsive to stimuli that might make us anxious that we will be hurt, rejected, or disappointed, and we constantly scan our environment for signs of some form of relational threat.

For CoAs, this can mean becoming hyperfocused on other people's expressions, expectations, needs, and possible next moves so that we can steer clear of trouble. This little fact is codependency in the making. We start to base our behavior on what we believe will fit best into the situation that we fear.

Chronic Stress. Because it causes the constant release of the stress hormone cortisol, chronic stress can get us stuck in our fight/flight/freeze response. Too much cortisol can cause stressful relating to morph into codependent relating by undermining the cortex's ability to regulate fear signals coming from the amygdala. Too much cortisol also partially shuts down the hippocampus, the part of the brain that helps us to accurately perceive and read our environment. The hippocampus's job is to provide context, to tell us what is scaring us and just how scared we need to be, and to ground us in our present-oriented environment. When this part of the brain is not functioning correctly, we can feel lost in space, and we feel like our anxiety, along with our need to control and fix, gets bigger.

So when the amygdala is firing too many fear signals and the hippocampus and cortex aren't working properly, we become simultaneously stressed out and unable to regulate our overwhelming stress. We can get stuck in the stress inside of us and unable to put what's us triggering into context in order to manage it. We overread or overreact to signals like mood shifts, change in vocal tones, or even another person's momentary insecurity. So we rush in to help, fix, control, or manage the person who is making us anxious. We mood manage them instead of ourselves in the mistaken perception that if we can just get them to change, we will feel calmer and less anxious.

Intimacy can get stuck right here. When partners, for example, are simultaneously in this state, no new information can get in and the "stuck place" that they're in can't get processed and put into context. Everything they feel is "about" someone else and they do not reflect on their own behavior, nor do they "hold" the couple dynamic in their minds very well.

Projecting Our Disowned Feelings onto Others. Codependency is not the same as selflessness. Selflessness is a choice. Parents are often called on to be selfless, putting their children's needs before their own, recognizing that their child's state of development requires this. But codependency is not a putting aside or postponing of personal need; it is a projection of personal need that we do not recognize within ourselves onto another person. It is a reaction to and a projection of the state we enter when we're anxious and hypervigilant. There is an old joke that goes, "A codependent is someone who puts a sweater on someone else . . . when they feel cold." In other words, codependents identify their own feelings in other people rather than within themselves and then they set about taking care of in another person what they truly need/want taken care of within themselves. In a sense, it's easier to focus on another person's feelings than their own. Codependents may have trouble identifying and owning their own feelings because they have had little practice or encouragement in doing so. Needless to say, this habit of identifying our own feelings in someone else while disowning them in ourselves complicates intimacy and parenting.

Boundaries: The Urge to Merge

It's difficult to have good boundaries when we're more aware of another person than we are of ourselves, or when we project our pain rather than own and process it. When we are more focused on scanning another person's emotional state than our own, we do several things: we may misread their emotions because our fear mind is the mind doing the reading. We may also have trouble distinguishing them from us; we feel not "for" them but "as" them. We tune in so much to the other that we lose ourselves in that person's feelings. We get confused, and when CoAs get confused, we don't like it and we want to fix it, fast! Unfortunately, this rarely works because as long as we're hypervigilant in our "reading" of another person, we are not clearly seeing them or ourselves.

Setting boundaries in an alcoholic/addicted home is not easy. After all, at least one parent is violating one of the most basic boundaries of parenting by being unfit and bringing no end of pain and fear into the household. Addicts violate the safety of the home and everyone in it, and that, along with all of the denial and deception that surround addiction, are fundamental boundary violations.

Women: Wired for Connection

Women are wired for connection from birth, and, in terms of codependency, this can be a liability. Nature has designed the female of the species to pick up on the subtle signals from others so that we can be sensitive caretakers of our young (Brazendine 2006). Robert Ackerman, author of *Perfect Daughters*, conducted a study in 1989; he found that "daughters of alcoholics reported a significantly higher need for control, over-reaction to change, and feelings of overresponsibility for others. They also rated themselves higher in difficulty with intimacy, approval and affirmation, and judging themselves harshly as compared to daughters of nonalcoholics. In an open-ended, follow-up survey, 33 percent of the adult daughters of alcoholics (versus 9 percent of the adult children of nonalcoholics) reported the greatest parenting issue for them as parents was their "need for control" (Ackerman 1988). They reported taking on too many responsibilities for their children by overprotecting them, had extremely high expectations of their children, and "felt responsible for making sure everything in the family was under control"(ibid).

Simply being aware of women's qualities of connection can allow women to manage this extra sensitivity; it is, after all, a gift of nature. Women's ability to pick up on subtle signals and read moods are beautiful qualities when understood. Our world has relied on that ability for centuries to bring tenderness and sensitivity into the home and toward children, and now, thankfully, that ability is finding its way into the workplace and the political arena.

Healing trauma is healing codependency. As historical pain is processed rather than projected and the self becomes more distinct and present oriented, codependent behaviors begin to clear up naturally.

NINE

The Narcissistic Parent: Disappearing Into Someone Else's Story

"The mother gazes at the baby in her arms, and the baby gazes at his mother's face and finds himself therein . . . provided that the mother is really looking at the unique, small, helpless being and not projecting her own expectations, fears, and plans for the child. In that case, the child would find not himself in his mother's face, but rather the mother's own projections. This child would remain without a mirror, and for the rest of his life would be seeking this mirror in vain."

—Donald Woods Winnicott

"I felt like it was all about them, like what was going on inside of me was sort of invisible, like what they wanted or needed always came first. We were just always tiptoeing around so we wouldn't set them off." ACoAs often describe family dynamics that circulate around the immediate needs of the addict. They talk about how they often found themselves staying quiet and "well-behaved" so as not to disturb a drunk or hungover parent. They also describe a world in which their other parent was stressed out and working double time to make the family seem "normal." Or they describe the opposite—a parent who had sort of collapsed into helplessness and left the job of parenting to whomever—if anyone—would fill in. Too much of the time, CoAs have limited access to not one but two parents.

Children are naturally needy. When they feel that there is no room for their needs because the parents' needs are sucking up all of the relationship oxygen, they develop circuitous ways of meeting their needs through others—codependency in the making. These kids often experience their parents' needs as more immediate and important than their own. Children tend to feel that they are disappearing around their narcissistic parents. The message is strong that their parents are the center of the universe.

Children learn that the way to connect with the narcissistic parent is to satisfy their needs first, so they subordinate their own needs to their parent's. They may idealize the narcissistic parent in order to gratify him or her, because they discover that it is a way to remain in that parent's favor. They may learn to not ask or even expect an attuned response to what they need, because asking and not getting what they are asking for is just too strange and it hurts, or they assume another person will not want to meet their needs. So they attempt to meet their needs privately, within themselves and by themselves. Eventually they may feel uncomfortable even having needs, and so they try to hide them, even from themselves; they shut down that feeling within them.

Their own inner worlds can feel hazy and confusing to them while the worlds of others seem clear and distinct.

Why Living with Addiction
Feels Like Living with Narcissism

The narcissist tends to view other people as extensions of himself, not necessarily as individuals in their own right. A narcissist often prefers to have people around him who behave in such a way as to meet and gratify his own needs or enhance his own vision of himself. If others act separately from him, have too many of their own points of view or their own opinions, they threaten the narcissist's equilibrium.

How does this mirror addiction? Addiction creates a kind of narcissism and self-absorption. It is constantly preoccupying; it takes over a person—body, mind, and soul. For those who live with an addict, love them, and depend on them to be at the other end of a relationship, life can be discouraging. It's a lot like living with a narcissist, because no matter what you do or how hard you try, you will always come second: second to the addict's pressing needs, second to their constant preoccupations, second to the disease.

Another scenario that can make CoAs feel alone is if the non-addict parent is narcissistic. When this is the case, children can have a very complicated time meeting their own needs because they have a lot of people to tend to first. They have two very self-absorbed, preoccupied parents.

An Underdeveloped Sense of Self

Both narcissism and addiction reflect immaturity. A narcissist has not made it through feeling and understanding his own needy childhood self and matured into a stage of development where he can actually feel his way into the world of another person and empathize with what he or she might feel. First of all, the narcissist does not necessarily know what he feels, and second, he can't reverse roles with other human beings and feel "as" them for just a brief moment and then return to his own self. While he can feel in the abstract for causes or large bodies of people, he has trouble feeling appropriately with the human being across the breakfast table. Narcissists are stuck somewhere along the developmental continuum in a place where what matters to them is to satisfy their needs first and foremost. Their needs, however, have an immature sort of flavor. Like a child who cannot see past his pressing need of the moment into what satisfying it might cost in terms of his relationships, the narcissist cannot really understand how to meet his own needs while in relationship with another person.

In this sense, narcissists are immature in a way similar to the way in which addicts are immature. Self-medication is self-destructive, and the person engaging in it is putting his own overpowering emotion before anything else. This reflects a self that cannot come up with more mature and functional ways of mood and pain management. Self-medicators have trouble tolerating their own neediness and pain, translating it into words, and processing it to get to the other side of it—as do narcissists. Both often take refuge in grandiose fantasies manipulating others as a way to shore up their sinking sense of self. The narcissist and the addict have a lot in common here, and in this way they may attract each other. The unspoken bargain may be that neither will call the other on their selfishness.

Wouldn't it be nice, we think, *to be free of this burden of awareness of the needs and feelings of others and simply ask ourselves one question. What do I want?* But if you peek inside the inner world of the narcissist or the addict, you might be startled at the emptiness and loneliness you'd find. Because ultimately, being oblivious to the cares and needs of others leaves narcissists as well as addicts feeling like strangers in their own relational worlds. Whatever they are doing to meet their needs isn't working all that well for the long run. And those who love a narcissist can feel the kind of helplessness, hurt, and rage that result from loving someone who cannot fully love them back.

The Narcissistic Parent

The narcissist views people as extensions of the self rather than separate beings with their own needs, drives, emotions, and personalities. The narcissist looks at people and thinks, *Where do they fit into my life? What can they do for me?* Children require attunement from a caring adult to learn to tune in on themselves, so having a narcissistic parent can be a lonely or even a shocking experience. In order not to feel so alone, these children may find themselves desperately trying to flatter, take care of, placate, or please their parent. They may be more pre-occupied with what will gratify their parent than with how they might amuse or please themselves in a effort to somehow share their parent's "space."

"I feel like I am just sort of there," says Jasmine, "like my feelings just don't matter. Basically I just sit and listen to my mom go on and on about herself. It's boring. The best I can hope for is that she might *refer* to me or say something *about* me, but she rarely talks *to* me, asks me questions, listens to the answers, and thinks on what I am saying. It's just always . . . all about her. She brags all the time about any dumb thing she might be doing. If she asks how I am, it's been so long since I've heard it that I can't even think of what to say, so she just keeps talking. It's *The Mom Show.*"

In her mother's presence, Jasmine feels invisible, bored, hurt, enraged. She wonders if her mother even remembers it is she on the other end of the phone. She doesn't dare to interrupt her mother's monologue because there seem to be no breaks in it, no room for another person. Her mother uses distancing language when she talks to Jasmine. She gets Jasmine's name wrong or acts as if she is not at all special. Because a child already feels, in a sense, "one down" to a parent's natural authority, such treatment can feel especially disempowering. With the narcissist, caring can feel like a one-way street: *I listen to you, I think about you, I hear, acknowledge, and understand you. But you do not feel obliged or motivated to do those things for me.* If Jasmine wants to share the light with her mom, well, the spotlight doesn't move so Jasmine has to. Jasmine can scoot into a corner of Mom's light and share some of it. But she doesn't get the light turned on her. That would leave Mom in the dark, at least in Mom's mind, and in Mom's mind, there is not enough light for everyone. For children, this can be an experience that constitutes a million small shocks to their system—little moments that gather strength over time and interfere with their own development of a sense of self.

There is nothing more important to the child than to be seen by the parent. When children cannot direct their parent's "sight" toward them when they want or need it and when they cannot feel "seen into" by their parent, they can feel deeply alone. They are left to make a Hobson's choice—that is, to choose between two equally bad options: To remain close to my mom, do I more or less put my own self on a shelf and simply adjust to being there for her? Or do I move away from her, risk not pleasing her, separate, and have her see me as a problem?

Narcissists can appear almost helpless or endearing in their need, and they can engender a wish in another person to take care of them; but if you do not fill their needs or take care of them as they wish, you will likely be dismissed because you are simply not doing your job of thinking about them. In this sense, the narcissist is the odd combination of fragile and aggressive.

One of the necessary steps of individuation from the parent is to be able to feel our own feelings *while* in the presence of the parent, to experience our own self as separate and distinct from our parent but still connected to him or her. The narcissist does not encourage a separate but connected relationship—you are part of their foreground or part of their background. They may think of you while you are in their presence, but you do not get the feeling that they carry thoughts of you around with them;

out of sight is out of mind. For these children, the relationship with the narcissistic parent may be a deeply hurtful and demoralizing experience. They feel that they can never be who they really are and be seen by their parent, that their parent will never really know them. And they are probably right. If you do not put a narcissistic parent first, he or she may experience it as a personal assault and will not necessarily accommodate your need to be autonomous; your actions may even be perceived as a threat.

Sibling Competition

Children of narcissists can become schooled in endless, subtle ways of pleasing their parents; they can feel proud, clever, and even superior to their siblings who cannot seem to get the idealizing role right. Rather than gaining a sense of self from their own estimable activities and relationships, they may gain a sense of self from being the chosen child, the one who understands how to stay close to Mom and how to please her. The child who pushes back, who says, "What about me? I'm here, too," may create unpopular waves.

When children have a feeling that their parent is there for them and can give them the love and attention that they crave when they need it—when a parent can respond in an attuned way, in other words—children can relax and feel like there is enough "parent love" to go around. When this is not the case, it can give rise to sibling competition.

Playing Favorites

Siblings may perceive (erroneously or correctly) that the narcissistic parent is playing favorites, which can leave some siblings feeling passed over or discounted. The favored child will often be the one who does not challenge the narcissist but gives him or her the demanded attention and adulation. The child has witnessed what happens to siblings who disagree with their parent. He or she may be loath to risk losing either the glow of the parent's approval and affection or the feeling of place and power that come from being chosen over other siblings.

The narcissistic parent may also play children off against each other, holding one sibling over the other—for example, saying, "I don't have this problem with so and so, just with you." Meeting his or her own needs is primary for this parent. If a child should talk about feeling hurt or passed over, the narcissist is likely to stare blankly or become irritated. Children in these situations may learn one of several things: to give up and feel that they will never please a narcissistic parent; to fight an endless fight in which their parent will always see them as "difficult" when they disagree; or to succumb and become the child that the narcissistic parent wants. In the third "solution," this child remains special and chosen but at the expense of his own individual sense of self.

Narcissism and Neurobiology:
Early Attachment and Self-Regulation

We pick up on the moods of others through the phenomenon

of limbic resonance. Our nervous systems extend beyond the borders of our bodies, they link with those of the people close to us in a silent, radiating rhythm that helps regulate everyone's physiology. Children require ongoing neural synchrony from parents in order for their natural capacity for self-directedness to emerge. In other words, it is through successful relationships that we achieve a healthy sense of autonomy. Human physiology does not direct all of its own functions, it is interdependent. It must be steadied and stabilized by the physical presence of another to maintain both physical and emotional health. "Limbic regulation mandates interdependence for social mammals of all ages, but young mammals are in special need of its guidance: their neural systems are not only immature but also growing and changing. One of the physiologic processes that limbic regulation directs, in other words, is the development of the brain itself and that means attachment determines the ultimate nature of a child's mind" (Lewis 2001). "The limbic system plays an important role in guiding the emotions that stimulate the behavior necessary for self-preservation and survival of the species. It is responsible for such complex behaviors as feeding, fighting, fleeing, and reproduction, and it also assigns free-floating feeling of significance, truth, and meaning to experience" (MacLean, 1985). "Destruction of parts of the limbic system abolishes social behavior, including play, cooperation, mating, and care of the young" (van der Kolk 2005).

Attachment literature could allow us to extrapolate that in their very early development, narcissists may not have had the quality of interaction and attunement from their caregivers that would have allowed them to develop a solid enough network of neurological wiring to become empathic. Their "we state" or *co-state* appears to be underdeveloped. If we see narcissism as related to early trauma or a primary attachment rupture, we could surmise that narcissists are left with a somewhat incomplete sense of attachment, that they experience their inner world as an internal emptiness or void that they cannot fully tune into, and therefore they have trouble tuning in on the internal states of others or mentally reversing roles with them. This can give narcissists a sort of superficial quality; Surfaces are important to narcissists; in an absence of a strong sense of an inner world that is connected to the inner worlds of those around them, the narcissist often seems to try to get things to "be right" by getting them to "look right."

Though narcissists may appear to be fiercely independent, on the inside they are forever searching for the kind of early attachment that would allow them to internalize the caring presence and energy of a love object so that they can feel whole on the inside. The road to a narcissist's heart is to admire them, to nourish them, to feed them. As a primary developmental need that was never met, it makes sense, but it is a problem for another adult because adult roles like partnering and parenting require that we are able to equally share a "we state," that we can be tuned in to another person and allow them to tune in on us. This state is neurologically wired in very early in development through the caring, attuned physical and emotional holding that goes on in a parent/child relationship. Being close to a narcissist may ask that we be willing to be swallowed and digested whole. This can be unpleasant for the "other" person.

Because the damage to the narcissist occurs in early years, it is my feeling that it profoundly affects the ability to be close and attuned but minimally affects intelligence. By the time narcissists are at the stage of intellectual development where their brain allows them to abstract, they are in school, learning and probably getting plenty of opportunities to grow. It is emotional learning that seems missing, not intellectual learning. This makes narcissists all the more confusing: they can think so clearly, piece together such seemingly attractive personnas, but the feeling connection is underdeveloped. In a relationship, this means that a narcissist can observe you, sometimes very perceptively, but does not tune into your inner world.

Will My Narcissistic Parent Ever Change?

It is not likely that narcissistic parents will change. Narcissists rarely get help as they cannot step away from themselves and see themselves through another person's eyes. Besides, they feel that they are fine; it is the rest of the world who is out of step. And if they do get help, it will have to be the "best" help possible and will likely be short lived. They remain true to the Greek myth about Narcissus, who fell in love with his own reflection and for whom this disorder was named.

Integrating the "Good" and "Bad" Parent

There is a moment in all children's lives when it dawns on them that their parent isn't perfect, a time when the disparity between the wished for, idealized parent of the innocent child mind needs to be integrated into a more realistic picture of who the parent really is—someone with personal limitations, foibles, and faults. Someone who is not perfect. Someone who can be loved in spite of imperfections. Melanie Klein, a psychoanalyst who was famous for work with and about children, refers to this moment in the child's life as "the depressive position" because even in the best of cases it is a loss of innocence and a profound shift in expectations—a disappointment. No longer can the child call on the magical, protective presence of the parent to make everything okay, to hold monsters at bay, to meet all needs, and to make pain and angst disappear.

Jean was a beautiful, bright, and privileged girl who had a special closeness with her alcoholic mother, who called her Jeannie. On the one hand, Jean was so welcome in her mother's inner sanctum that she came to terms with many of her mother's weaknesses earlier than her other siblings. She saw clearly her mother's self-absorption, but the little girl in her was still and forever enchanted with the magical feeling of being her mother's confidante. She was as much a mother to her mother as her mother was a mother to her. If that sentence is confusing, imagine how confusing the actual experience was. Jeannie hovered somewhere between knowing her mother's faults with amazing clarity and clinging to her idealized imaged of her mother. She had trouble integrating the beautiful woman who looked so elegant in Chanel suits and Ferragamo shoes, who knew how to entertain and make guests feel so at home at dinner parties, with the woman who could not walk a straight line down the bedroom hallway, who fell over on the dance floor, who was drunk and slurred her words at the family holiday party, and who quietly went to bed, took the phone off the hook, and pulled down the shades. And so Jean never did. Instead, she married a man who drank too much himself, telling herself all the same emotional lies that she learned as a child: *He is so good with people. He thinks I am so special. He will fit so naturally into my life, my family, my dreams. Our dreams.*

All children are faced with the task of integrating conflicting sides of the parents they love. For the child of addiction, this inner picture looks more like Picasso in his Cubist period than a Renoir. CoAs and ACoAs are faced with incorporating a drunken, out-of-control, and perhaps abusive parent into their internalized working model. If they have idealized their addicted parent in an attempt to ward off the despair and depression of seeing their parent's dark side, they also may feel that they are giving up an ideal parent or an ideal childhood along with it. Facing up to the very significant deficits of an alcoholic parent, or for that matter the enabling or narcissistic parent, can leave CoAs or ACoAs with a sense of loneliness and disappointment. It can feel like too great a task to undertake. But they need to integrate the good and bad parent so they don't project their shadow onto their spouses and children.

Children of fairly regulated parents have the job of facing up to their parents' faults, perhaps their tempers, or their shyness, weaknesses, or lack of success in the world. These children have to somehow incorporate these deficits into the image of the parents they have internalized throughout their childhood . . . the parents who seemed to have enchanted powers in a good-night kiss, who made the best-tasting food in the entire world, who lifted them into the air and into a heaven of two filled with blue sky, love, and warm, caressing breezes. Children need to make peace with their childhood wishes and their need to see their parents as all-powerful and perfect, and move into a more mature psychological state in which they can love their parents as they are, warts and all. There is a profound freedom in realizing that a parent isn't perfect, because we simultaneously incorporate the knowledge that we, too, can lead a relatively happy life, even without being perfect ourselves.

PART III:

Faces and Voices of the ACoA Trauma Syndrome

We have not even to risk the adventure alone, for the heroes
of all time have gone before us. The labyrinth is thoroughly known.
We have only to follow the thread of the hero path,
and where we had thought to find an abomination, we shall
find a god. And where we had thought to slay another, we
shall slay ourselves. Where we had thought to travel outward,
we will come to the center of our own existence. And where
we had thought to be alone, we will be with all the world.

—Joseph Campbell, *The Power of Myth*

TEN

Self-Medication: Misguided Attempts at Mood Management

*There is no greater agony than bearing
an untold story inside you.*

—Maya Angelou

Many addicts, whether they self-medicate with drugs, alcohol, food, sex, or spending, are ACoAs. Just as someone with a physical injury can become addicted to the medications that bring them relief from their chronic physical pain, an ACoA can become addicted to the "pain meds" (alcohol, drugs, food, sex, money) that bring them relief from their chronic emotional pain. When ACoAs cannot cope with the pain they are in, they often reach for some sort of mood-altering substance or behavior to do that for them.

The habit of self-medication can start very early. One of the misconceptions about addiction is that when the substance is removed, the addict's troubles are over. But we don't learn what our pain is trying to teach when we silence its voice. Addictions to mood-altering substances such as alcohol and/or drugs are called substance addictions. Addictions to mood-altering behaviors or activities, such as sex, eating, spending, and/or gambling, among others, are called process addictions.

Making Recovery Real: Sandy's Story

"I know I look together on the outside," Sandy says, "but on the inside, I feel like I'm falling apart." I observe this elegant young man as he dialogues with an empty chair and struggles to find the words to describe what has been festering inside of him, unarticulated and unspoken, for so long.

"Who are you?" Sandy asks the empty chair as he begins his role play. He is talking to that little boy who lives inside of him, the one he still wants to shove down. "I can't even find you. No, that's not really true. I don't *want* to find you. I'm ashamed of you. I don't want to look at you." He lifts a flat hand of rejection toward the chair that is representing the part of himself that he buried in a bucket of ice cream, then later in six packs of beer, and eventually in drugs. His inner child . . . adolescent . . . teenager.

"I just look at you and . . ." At this point he drops his head into his hands, and tears begin to flow down his cheeks. "I know how lonely you are, how different you feel, and I want to say I'm sorry. God, I'm so sorry that I stomped you down for so long, that I fed you drugs instead of food, that I dragged you to all those dark places. I'm sorry that I ignored and hurt you and made fun of you just the way they did to me. I'm sorry I hated you. I look in the mirror and I see you staring out at me."

As I watch his drama unfold, I am stunned. I am a therapist. I deal with this every day and still, these moments of self-disclosure take my breath away. What is it that makes us so vulnerable when we are small? How can it be that we don't forget about all of this: the old complexes about being left out of family conversation at the dinner table, humiliated or criticized by a father, or ignored by a mother whose love we want so desperately? How can this stay with us all our lives? Why do we want to hide from our needy sides that yearn for love, connection, and attention—indeed, from our basic humanness?

Sandy is well-groomed, well-educated, and from a well-heeled, liberal Boston Brahmin family. He first came to see me when he was thirty-seven, a year or so after a serious breakup with the woman he planned to marry. When his engagement ended, he felt as alone as he'd ever felt; vulnerable and in need of a way out. With his very social friends, that "out" was easily found; there was always a house to go to and a place to party well into the night after all the other parties had broken up. Those who felt so inclined could sniff and smoke and drink their way into oblivion—in style and comfort. Drugs and alcohol provided Sandy with not only immediate relief from emotional pain but also a ready group of loyal comrades to keep him company—until, of course, he got sober. Then all the music and laughter stopped, and he felt alone with just the relentless pounding of his own heart to fill the void in which he found himself.

The Trigger Event Relationship

"I thought we would always be together," said Sandy about his fiancée. "I really loved her and I let myself trust her, but I pushed her away."

Thinking back on when Sandy first started working with me, I recall that his breakup had clearly plunged him into overwhelming and confusing pain. It also turned what was previously social, diversionary drinking and occasional pot-smoking into full-blown addiction. Sandy's problems with full-blown addiction were short-lived; his pattern of self-medication, so common among ACoAs, had deeper roots. Unknowingly, Sandy had been trying to drown the pain not only of his breakup, but the deeper, earlier losses that were now getting triggered and mixed up with his present pain.

More backstory . . . let's look back at when I began seeing Sandy; his intake went something like this:

"Do you drink much, Sandy, or do other drugs?" I asked.

"No, not really," said Sandy, raising his hand to his chin in reflection and leaning back in his chair. "I party with my friends on weekends but I don't get out of control. We all indulge." He rolled his eyes slightly, which I wasn't sure how to interpret.

"Would you say that you drink when you're feeling depressed?"

"No, mostly socially, when I go out."

"Do you ever drink or drug alone?" I asked.

"No, always with my friends, only when I'm out," said Sandy. "But I can always stop. I don't think alcohol or drugs are my problem. I think it's this other stuff—that stuff from when I was a little kid that I can't seem to get at."

It was hard to tell how much Sandy had been using drugs and alcohol to numb the pain of losing his fiancée and their plans for a future together. One indication that this might be the case was that he couldn't move through the anguish from his breakup, but I believed him when he said that his main issues were related to CoA trauma. Sandy came to group but found connecting difficult, and it became evident after a few groups that he would need to abstain from drugs and alcohol in order to process feelings. Yet he was not ready to admit this to himself.

When Sandy missed a group, no one was too surprised. "I got a call from London," he said. "I think I may have missed a group. I've met a girl. I really have to give this a chance. I haven't felt this way in a long time. I won't be there this next week either."

The next week I got another call: "Missing another group, so sorry, things taking a little longer than expected . . . work possibility I need to check out, hope you can understand, apologize to everyone, see you next week. . . ."

His next communication was by e-mail: "Please forgive my unexcused absence. I know I committed to a year in group. I'm just not sure this process is, well, working for me at the moment. I'm feeling a lot better. I think the work is so important, but I just don't think I'm ready for it, just not right now. Sometime, though. I know I need to do it." He was doing the whole thing all over again, re-creating his painful history of loving and losing in a matter of weeks. He was falling in love, breaking up, drinking and drugging to get over it. It was the same script, just accelerated. But unlike so many who start and stop recovery, Sandy wasn't blaming the group or me for why he was leaving.

He made it clear that he felt he needed to do this work but that he wasn't ready. That was actually very sane—maybe ambivalent and fraught with anxiety, but sane. And also kind and well-related: he did not wish to hurt or alienate anyone. He needed to get to know himself, but he already knew a lot.

Six months later I heard from him again. "I'm sober. I've been sober for six months. I know I need this work. Will you let me back in group?" I asked him if he was going to AA.

"No, I tried a couple of meetings, but I don't know, they're just not for me." Even though this was a phone call, I could almost see him wincing. "The God stuff—I just can't get into it. And I don't need it to stay sober."

"If you come back to group, you will need to go to AA."

"I'll give another meeting a try. I can't promise anything; I want to be honest."

"Sorry, if you come back to group you need to be in AA and seeing a therapist one-on-one. You need safe places to process all the feeling that will inevitably come up as we examine what's underneath your self-medicating, why you wanted to drink and drug in the first place."

"I thought once I got sober I'd feel so much better, but I feel worse."

"You're feeling the pain that used to make you want to pick up and use."

"I don't like it."

"I know, no one really does."

"I feel like I got my appendix out and the medication is wearing off and it hurts like hell."

"You were medicating your emotional pain with drugs and alcohol. Now you're sober. You're feeling it."

"I thought when I got sober it wouldn't hurt anymore."

"I know."

"So can I come back to the group?"

"I need to check it out with everyone, to make sure they are willing to reinvest in your recovery, Sandy. You disappeared, remember? Groups don't like that much. Can you give me a few days?"

"I'll think about it."

"You think about it."

Six weeks later I got another call. Sandy was going to two to three meetings a week and willing to go to more if his emotions got rocky. He'd find a therapist. Did I have any recommendations?

"I just know I need this work. It's the only thing that feels hopeful to me. I'm not worried about relapsing. Sobriety is okay, but I'm emotionally relapsing, if that makes any sense. I'm all over the place."

"Welcome back, Sandy. I'll see you on Monday."

The Bottom of the Iceberg

As he was growing up, Sandy spent the bulk of his time with a young Irish nanny named Deirdre whom he grew to adore. His memories of her plunge him into a mixture of feelings both divine and downhearted. "I just remember being this happy little kid with her. I'm sure I wanted to be with my mother, but honestly, I was completely bonded to Deirdre. Sometimes I wonder

if I thought she was my mother. She was just this warm, loving, wonderful woman." In his mind, Deirdre was his first love.
His own mother had returned to a high-powered business job so
quickly after Sandy's birth that he hardly knew her. As a new-
born, Sandy had enough bonding chemicals coursing through
his little brain and body to ensure an attachment powerful
enough to hold him to his birth mother until maturity. But the
woman he primarily bonded with was Deirdre. Still, this was
okay. He was getting what he needed to develop a sound little
emotional infrastructure, to feel loved and valued. He adored his
surrogate mommy, and the feelings were mutual. He belonged
somewhere and to someone. He felt happy and whole.

The real trouble for Sandy began when his mother "suddenly"
realized that her now-four-year-old son was much more attached
to Deirdre than he was to her. "My mother just came home and
fired Deirdre one day. She took six months off and *poof*, Deirdre
was gone, no more, like she'd died or something." This traumatic
rupture forced Sandy to attempt to re-bond, however anxiously,
to his own mother. "I was getting the person I'd probably wanted
in the first place, but I was always so anxious she'd leave, I guess,
so I literally clung to her. Maybe I missed Dierdre, too, I must
have. If my mom had stayed, it would probably all have been
fine; I loved her."

But in six months, partly because of money pressures, and
perhaps feeling smothered by motherhood and seeing her own
chances at a career slip away, his mother sent Sandy off to kin-
dergarten and returned to work. Sandy had "lost" two mothers
in the space of six months. And his father was slipping further

into an alcohol addiction. Sandy returned each day from school to a housekeeper who was preoccupied with cooking and cleaning and had little time for him. His mother returned home most nights for a late dinner, but he spent very little time with her. He did, however, have his brother, Malcolm, seven years his senior, who then became his salvation and his hero. But eighteen months later Malcolm, who he worshipped and tagged around with every afternoon, joined their other brother Freddie at boarding school. No one really prepared Sandy for Malcolm's departure or helped him find activities to fill his now empty afternoons.

Sandy lost access to his two mommies and Malcolm all in the space of three years. Sadly, the magnitude of these losses didn't register with any of the adults around him. They didn't recognize that he had lost anything at all. Acting as though nothing had changed, Sandy was told by his parents to come home from school, do his homework, and wait for them to have dinner. But he couldn't concentrate on anything; the words swam in front of his eyes. Sandy's parents tried to keep the trouble that was brewing within their own relationship from showing. When Sandy tried to reach out for some kind of help, he was told that everything was all very fine, that he was the only problem. He needed to study harder, be a better boy, stop worrying. To make life even more isolating, he lived far away from all of his friends and couldn't solve his loneliness by passing his afternoons at other people's houses.

So Sandy did what most kids do: he found a childlike way out of his emptiness. "I just dug into cartons of ice cream that I swiped from the kitchen when the housekeeper wasn't looking.

Sometimes I stole candy from other kids or from the corner store. I obliterated my feelings with sweets. When I was supposed to be doing my homework, I just sat there stuffing my face and watching TV in the dark, then I'd race out of the room when I heard my parents come home." This is when Sandy's pattern of self-medicating began; treats and TV became his solace, and the gulf between himself and his parents widened. The gulf between himself and his real feelings widened, too.

Sandy and his parents ate dinner together most nights, though it was rather late for Sandy. At the dinner table, which perhaps could have offered a place for reconnection at the end of the day, Sandy just found more isolation. His brothers were gone and his parents were tired and preoccupied, barely paying any attention to him and probably avoiding talking about anything because talking about anything might lead to talking about everything, which could lead to breaking apart the whole lie they were living. Then what would happen? His mother was invested in maintaining appearances and being the center of attention, while his father was invested in not being called on his increasing alcohol use. Sandy sank further into his little hole.

"I remember sitting at the table one night and I was just so excited. I'd hit a game-winning home run against our rival school—and I mean I wasn't that great at baseball 'cause I was sort of a fat kid. I spent more time on the bench then playing, but the coach gave me a shot at the end of this game and I'd hit this home run. The whole team made a big deal out of it—it was a huge moment for me; I went from outcast to hero. It made me so happy and I was so excited to tell my parents."

"Were they at the game?" I asked.

"I didn't even think of that. No, they weren't. And at dinner, I waited until my mother had told us about her day and then, when she finally asked me about mine, I gushed about it, telling them every detail. My dad tried to say some nice things and my mom just barely heard it. It was like a, 'Oh good, pass the salt,' kind of thing. I remember running to my room and being so upset and they didn't even know why. They were just so not tuned into me; I was just this kid running around their house. I think I just gave up ever trying to connect with them or please them after that." Like so many CoAs, Sandy thought he was the problem. He had no idea that his parents had problems they were barely managing.

When Sandy turned thirteen, what felt like a minor miracle occurred. "I just went from being this pudgy, short kid to being the height I am now, six feet three inches, and thin, and suddenly good-looking (he blushes). It was so great in some ways. I mean, it was incredible, but in another way it pushed this hurting kid inside of me even further down, you know what I mean?"

The pressure was now on through his teenage years. He became much more athletic, a better student, and had many friends, both male and female. "But now, maybe because I finally looked like I was supposed to, my parent's expectations *really* kicked in. I tested super-high, so everyone knew I was smart, but I still couldn't concentrate. I was sort of split—big on the outside but this screaming little kid was still on the inside. And because I was now expected to do so well, I had this constant thing hanging over me, nipping at my heels. I had such high expectations but no one to support me, to teach me how to get there. So I became super anxious about failing. And I had this recurring nightmare that I'd wake up one day and be this freckled-faced, fat kid all over again. I guess that's when I found pot and alcohol. I just wish I'd had someone—anyone—to talk to. Every time I tried to talk to my mom she just told me I was fine, and my dad tried to understand, but, I don't know, he just didn't really stand up for me or for himself or for anyone, really. I just pushed it all further down and thought there was something wrong with me that couldn't be fixed. I just blamed myself and got high and hid it from my parents—which wasn't really all that hard."

Sandy walked around feeling like a wounded little boy submerged in the body of a handsome young man. He was hurting and confused inside with no one to help him with it, so he came up with his own solution, a way to make his anxiety more manageable. Food wasn't working anymore, so he looked for something stronger; drugs and alcohol did the trick. Not only did they soothe and quiet his fears but they gave him the sense of confidence that he lacked. They made him feel capable of facing his life. They gave him a false sense of feeling full instead of empty, calm instead of anxious, social instead of withdrawn, and happy instead of sad. But when the effects of the substances eventually and inevitably wore off, he'd crash and have to face reality. The painful feelings he had temporarily numbed would re-emerge, only they would be even more confusing and disturbing to him now because of this constant cycling between false confidence and gaiety back to sad and lonely. And physically he felt increasingly lousy after using, which really intensified all of his bad feelings. So the next time he'd need even more alcohol and drugs to make his feelings go away again. Thus began his dance of addiction. His only way to attain emotional comfort was through synthetic means; he had no idea how to get there on his own.

Breaking the Chain: The ACoA Under the Addict

Today Sandy successfully abtains from drugs and alcohol, but the emotions that he used to manage with them are confusing and difficult for him to deal with since he's had little practice to date. For starters, it's hard for him to even distinguish one feeling from another: hurt quickly turns into rage, frustration into hopelessness, and excitement into high anxiety or preoccupation. Once these feelings get hold of him, he tends to become easily overwhelmed and frightened by the intensity of his own, somewhat unfamiliar feelings. Drugs and alcohol used to be his emotional brakes; now he doesn't have them.

Sandy's situation is typical of addicts during their first year of sobriety. When the initial thrill of abstinence wears off, the realities of life sink in, and old, unfelt ACoA-related emotions reassert themselves. Sandy's sobriety was well-established. Now began the recovery process from his ACoA/PTSD issues. He began reconnecting with the child—the screaming little, hurt, and vulnerable kid living inside of him.

"I'm so sorry I tried to forget about you and pushed you back into the depths of my memory, that I tried to pretend you don't exist. I get now that this is exactly what everyone else did to you all along and must have made you hurt even more and made you feel even more forgotten and alone. I didn't want to hear your screaming in the dark. I didn't want to know about how much you hurt inside, but now I want to change that. I want to protect you and help you feel good about yourself, to calm the hurricane of emotion you always felt but could never express. You tried for so long to do this on your own, but it was like building a foundation on quicksand, and you were always sinking back into it. Those days are over: you are not crazy. I am here now, and I'm going to help you find solid ground."

Don't worry, Sandy, I think as I sit here, *you will be okay. You will know a freedom you have never known before. You will find yourself. And in finding yourself you will find everything else.*

Your life is waiting for you. Go get it.

Frozen Feelings: Fear and Trauma

It can be difficult to access trauma "memories" through reflective talking alone (van der Kolk 2004). For this reason I find psychodrama, which allows memory to emerge through action and role-play, an ideal form of therapy for trauma resolution if done simply and with no "script" or agenda coming from the therapist. Role play accesses the limbic world, the world of powerful emotions and imagery that is pressing to come forward. We cannot describe what we cannot feel.

When someone who has walled off his feelings is asked to "tell his trauma story," he might stare blankly, he might try to come up with a story, or even worse, might adopt a therapist's story as his own. He might be put into the embarrassing position of freezing all over again. He is at risk for telling a story that is not grounded in his own feeling and relevant, personal meaning. A story that therefore never gets experienced and processed remains intellectual and repetitive. He gets stuck in his own story but the exit door alludes him. Role play does not put someone in that bind; it simply says, "say what you'd like to say to so and so," the story pours forward, and words are found along with relevant emotion as meaning becomes clear. The limbic system operates with split-second speed; we're designed to feel first and think second. Role play works with this natural flow and allows for the feeling and sensory story—the limbic story—to emerge first and then be translated into language; thus feeling, thought, and sense impressions integrate easily. Role play immerses the being in his own experience, and while being in it, he finds his own way out of it, and the brain as well as the body forms new neural wiring, their own path out of pain, that frees him from the repetitive, recycling encapsulated trauma mind trap.

This is how it works for allowing historical pain to emerge. In normal day-to-day living, we also experience feelings faster than thoughts. But once we're aware of what we're feeling, our thinking mind becomes our best friend. Through awareness, we can gain balance and insight and make choices based on our understanding of needs, wishes, goals, and our self.

Sandy's emotion came up much more naturally talking to an empty chair representing a part of him than trying to find adult words to describe frozen child feelings. Though he is amazingly articulate, there is more immediate emotion that emerges in a role-play talking "to" himself than if he were talking "about" himself. It is more immediate and direct and has the added benefit of beginning and strengthening an inner dialogue between his adult self and his child self. Then, when I invited Sandy to reverse roles and momentarily *become* his child self, he had greater access to the words because he was, in fact, sitting in the feelings and the role of his inner child. As Sandy allows the child feelings to emerge, his adult mind looks on or "witnesses" and he is able to look at himself with new, more compassionate and mature eyes. He is able to take his child self by the hand to walk slowly with him toward maturity. He takes this innocent, lively, and creative part of himself with him instead of leaving him behind, frozen and mute.

Progress Toward Emotional Sobriety

Sandy's first year of sobriety can only be described as tumultuous. He arrived each Monday at group alternately feeling elated or desperate and confused; all of the emotions that he had been medicating for years were crowding in on him and he felt overwhelmed and burdened by them—but he had hope and he had commitment.

Many evenings, Sandy was filled with rage and recrimination for his parents, for his siblings, and for himself. It was amazing to observe him try to hold onto himself while he experienced what he called "the hurricane," the swirl of intense emotions that used to feel so overwhelming that he ate, drank, and drugged them away. He literally held onto his chair and winced as those foreign feelings pushed their way toward the surface of his mind. He had been so used to silencing them that feeling them represented a strange, new world.

What is happening from the trauma point of view is that the body and mind are caught in an interplay that make us feel that we're spinning into a black hole. The disturbing and sometimes painful body sensations (heart pounding or tightness, sweating, shortness of breath, dry throat, and so on) that accompany anxiety and fear trigger feelings and fragments of trauma-related imagery—scary scenes. Then the scary mental pictures that are racing through your mind trigger more disturbing body sensations and emotions. This becomes an internal combustion that can become explosive. It's why learning the skills of deep breathing, relaxing, and slowing down are so important. Guided imagery and meditating can be very helpful here, along with sane forms of exercise. Sandy took up meditation, painting, walking, and racquetball. In his second year of sobriety, he bought a dog and fell in love with her.

As I work with Sandy, I have the sensation that I am watching a child grow up and discover the world as he experiences both the joy and terror of growth. And as I witness the transformation, I ask myself, *How did we get here? How did this young man turn from brooding and self-destructive (albeit always with his intelligence and humor intact) to this amazingly sweet, balanced, and engaging guy?* Then I remind myself that the magic isn't in any one moment or any one insight, but in a symphony of small moments, of small insights that weave themselves together into a new picture, a new, integrated body/mind story, and thus a new body to live in.

It is dazzling, really, and very moving to be a part of someone's awakening into his own being and his shaping a new version of himself. Over the second year of Sandy's sobriety, I have found it remarkable and inspiring to watch him take hold of his inner world and reshape it. He has prioritized his physical and emotional sobriety and adopted the necessary life changes to make it real. While Sandy used to fidget in his chair, tap his hands and feet, and shift position constantly, now he sits at ease, limbs long and fluid. While his legs and feet used to turn in with tension and fear, now they stretch out in ease and comfort. His limbic system is healing before my eyes, and his body tells of a different man living inside of it. Sandy used to have a somewhat brooding, dark expression cast across his handsome young face. Now he is open and cheerful. He has a ready laugh; his humor often penetrates to the quick and is always welcome with group members, who he regularly sends into gales of laughter. His insights are unusually perspicacious for a man his age. He is able to wrap his mind around complex personal and interpersonal issues and translate them into words in a way that is worthy of a mature and deep person. He is developing the ability to marshal his excellent mind and bring his powers of observation within his control. Because of his hard work in recovery and his willingness to make significant and healthy lifestyle changes, Sandy has greatly accelerated his personal growth. He has changed in time so that he can alter the course of his life.

ELEVEN

Process Addictions: The Many Other Faces of Self-Medication

If you can't get what you want, you end up doing
something else, just to get some relief. Just to keep
from going crazy. Because when you're sad enough,
you look for ways to fill you up.

—Laura Pritchett, *Sky Bridge*

Everyone has some version of occasional self-medication. Richie has a beer to wind down after facing bumper-to-bumper traffic on the commute home. Tina misses her mother who lives in a city far away, so she eats a big bowl of macaroni and cheese because it reminds her of home. Lauren goes shopping to cheer herself up after a breakup with the guy she's been dating. But when does self-medicating turn from a harmless, occasional pick-me-up into a long-term problem with physical, emotional, and financial consequences?

Self-medicating takes hold when we compulsively use a

substance or behavior to manage and control moods and mental states that we cannot cope with on our own. It happens like this: We have a desire to feel better, and we discover that a certain action leads to the satisfaction of that desire. The more consistently that particular action leads to the state we want to achieve, the more we want to do it. Alcohol and drugs are common mood managers. They are reliable. We learn how many drinks or which drugs work best to achieve the result we want. We prescribe our own dose so to speak—we self-medicate.

When we don't understand how certain substances and behaviors play with our body chemistry and set us up for addiction, we're at risk for perpetuating lifestyles that slip into self-medication. We get stuck in hidden addictions.

Compulsive behaviors take hold in the brain because they are highly rewarded; they work with our own brain chemistry to make us feel good, but when we overuse these feel-good chemicals we can head straight into process addictions.

Dopamine, for example, is made in the brain and associated with feeling happy and chatty. It makes us feel calm and connected, smoothing out the rough edges. Food and certain behaviors like sex can also work to alter brain chemistry because they can have an analgesic effect similar to drugs or alcohol. According to Bart Hoebel, a psychologist at Princeton University, "Highly palatable foods and highly potent sexual stimuli are the only stimuli capable of activating the dopamine system (reward circuitry of the brain) with anywhere near the potency of addictive drugs" (Hoebel 2008). But then the crash comes. When dopamine levels drop after a food binge or orgasm, depression sets in and then we need more food or more sex to get the burst of mood-altering dopamine back. Certain foods affect dopamine levels, and when we overuse them we're taking that first step toward a process addiction. Sugar and the taste of sweets, for example, stimulate the brain by activating beta-endorphin receptor sites (ibid). These are the same chemicals activated by heroin and morphine. This is thought to be one of the drivers of compulsive overeating.

How Moments of Panic Lead to Self-Medication

Why does a gambler, in just a few minutes' time, burn through his child's college fund or lose the family home? Why does a compulsive eater drive through the night to find an open deli where she can load up on sugar and white flour and then try to throw it all up an hour later? What drives a sex addict to humiliate himself and his family and put all that he loves and has worked for at risk? What factors contribute to this mind-boggling loss of impulse control?

We all have a mind/body chemistry designed to nourish, sustain, and keep us safe. When that body chemistry gets thrown out of balance through trauma we have suffered or trauma we've brought onto ourselves, it can drive the kinds of behaviors that get us into trouble.

Engaging in risky behaviors can cause us to go into a fear/panic state. Here's how that cycle kicks in:

When our panic button gets pushed, our emergency systems engage; they go into fight/flight.

Then, our thinking mind (pre-frontal cortex), which is the part of us that perceives future consequences, goes off-line. We freeze in our tracks.

But our emotional (limbic) mind swings into high gear. In that moment of panic, we become all feeling with little or no thought. Oftentimes, in the case of process addictions, it's our own risky, acting-out behavior that scares us, behavior that may be fueled not only by old pain and a wish to get rid of it, but by fear of our actions of the moment. The food we don't want anyone to know we crave and have to have now! The sex we don't want anyone to know about because it could get us into huge trouble with our spouse. The spending that will leave us without money left to pay bills. These "crazy" high-risk behaviors can, and probably should, send us into a panic/shame spiral. That fear presses our panic button; we get flooded with awful feelings of shame and pain (what did I just do?) along with prickly, anxiety-provoking body sensations that make us all jumpy inside. Then there we are, in need of something to make us feel better fast. And we know what that is because we just did it. So we'll just do it again, this one last time. And it isn't all that bad anyway, it's just food, or sex, or one drink, or a little something we'd just love to take home, or one last win. And it's only just this once.

Emotional Eating: Feeding Our Feelings

It is estimated that fourteen million people are affected by an obsessive, compulsive, or disordered relationship with food. Jenni Schaeffer, author of *Life Without Ed: How One Woman Declared Her*

Independence from Her Eating Disorder, wrote a gripping piece that offers an unobstructed window into the mind of someone with disordered eating patterns. Jennie's words illustrate how chasing her own dopamine high to avoid feeling her depression led her down a desperate path toward a compulsive relationship with food.

> *After restricting food for days, I really needed energy. I dared to try an apple. I knew this would lead to eating more and more. Of course, it did. I started baking and bingeing. . . . I drove to a vending machine at my apartment complex, and it was empty. So I drove my car to a nearby convenience store at 2:00 AM. Would it still be open? How much money would I have to spend? Realizing I did not have enough money or my cell phone, I went back to my apartment to get both. Then I drove twenty minutes to a fast-food restaurant that is open twenty-four hours. I ordered lots of food at the drive-through and ate it in less than thirty seconds. A guy came running out of the store yelling something at me. Did he know what I was doing? . . . I know it's not safe driving in my car at 2:30 AM with a missing a headlight and a bad engine. But I drove to another fast-food restaurant to get more food. What is wrong with me? I wouldn't even eat dinner with Amy earlier today. But now, all I can do is eat. I have no control. I still need more food, but I can't go back to the same drive-through. They will recognize me. So I drive—now at 3:30 AM—forty-five minutes to a twenty-four hour grocery store. I buy lots of food that I had avoided eating earlier in the week. (I bought the exact candy that my boyfriend had offered to me and that I had refused.) My binges always equal everything I normally won't let myself touch at all.*
>
> *Finally, I am satisfied. That anxious feeling is gone. I drive home. I*

try to throw up twice. (I'm never very successful at this.) I am depressed.

I feel isolated from my mom and dad, Amy, my boyfriend, and every-
one. I don't want anyone to ask me about my eating. I have to avoid
everyone so that they won't ask. How did it get like this? I feel fat. I
don't want to eat again. My life is unmanageable because of food. But
what do I do? I feel helpless and fat. I can't break the cycle. I just want
to break the cycle.

I know what I can do. I won't eat tomorrow (Schaeffer 2012).

A study from Scripps Research Institute headquartered in La
Jolla, California, and published in *Nature Neuroscience* on March 28,
2010, found that junk food, or foods high in white sugar, white
flour, and unsaturated fats, can be as addictive to the brain as
cocaine, as it causes similar changes in the brain and sets up cravings for more junk food. In lab tests, rats given unlimited access
to high-calorie foods like candy bars and cheesecake not only
became obese very quickly, they continued gorging even when
this binging behavior led to an electric shock. Obese rats that
had their junk food replaced with a healthy diet actually stopped
eating completely because the reward system in the rats' brains
changed when they became compulsive eaters. "What we're seeing in our animals is very similar to what you'd see in humans
who overindulge," says lead researcher Paul J. Kenny, an associate professor of molecular therapeutics at the institute. "It seemed
that it was okay, from what we could tell, to enjoy snack foods,
but if you repeatedly overindulge, that's where the problem comes
in" (Johnson and Kenny 2010). Repeated indulgence in junk food
changes the brain chemistry to want that soothing, oblivious

high, or what amounts to self-medicating, so that the brain and body actually become locked into an addictive cycle that is similar to that of a cocaine addict.

Compulsive Combos: Invisible Addictions

One bad choice leads to another. Sugary foods can become a gateway to self-sabotaging food choices that can lead us straight into compulsive eating. ACoAs who don't want to think of themselves as alcoholics or drug addicts may be unwittingly manipulating their own body chemistry. Foods that contain sugar and white flour that the body immediately converts into sugar, along with a couple of drinks of alcohol that add to and potentate the sugar effect, constitute a "compulsive combo" that can become extremely addictive.

Holistic nutrition counselor Meredith Watkins writes about how food sets up cravings and increases anxiety levels that lead to self-medicating. "The recovering alcoholic who keeps a daily cocktail of caffeine and nicotine coursing through his veins and keeps white pasta and bagels on regular rotation in his diet . . . not surprisingly has alcohol cravings going through the roof. . . . In this case, the sugar from the white flour products acts in his body in the exact same way alcohol does." And the caffeine he is drinking with the bagel or muffin "is blocking the production of natural serotonin," his body's natural mood stabilizer (2012).

In her book *The Mood Cure*, Julia Ross talks about the chemical action of sugar and alcohol in an alcoholic's body: "Alcohol acts just like sugar biochemically, only more so. It contains more calories per gram, and it gets into your bloodstream faster. For people whose blood sugar levels tend to be low (of which research states that 95% of alcoholics are hypoglycemic), this can be irresistible" (2002). "This is why those bagels should be *verboten* to a recovering alcoholic" (Watkins 2012).

Sex Addiction: Living a Double Life

Mina,
I'm joy that I have a chance to get closer with u.
Friends call me Ira. I like sport, music, and Internet.
I've got shiny smile and attractive body.
Write me.
I saw your photos, and I wanna meet you.
Bye!

This was on fourteen-year-old Mina's computer when she logged on—some weird, Google-translated solicitation that no young girl should have to deal with, along with countless ads using pornographic language to advertise for Viagra, Cialis, and other similar meds.

Mina's parents are divorced. Her mother works long hours, and her father lives a long distance from her. Feeling lonely, she has gotten into the habit of visiting chat rooms. She met a "boy" online. They got close. Mina felt Don understood her, and he always seemed to ask the right questions. She got into the habit of spending hours each evening chatting with Don. His voice was warm and made her feel secure and cared about. After weeks of becoming closer than she had ever felt to anyone in her life, they decided to meet. When Mina met Don she was taken aback—he seemed much older than he said he was. She felt like a girl and like he was a much older man. Still, she was meeting her best friend. She felt scared, she felt confused, she felt betrayed. But she checked into a motel with him because they were so "close." After one visit, she told her mother.

A statistic from the Society for the Advancement of Sexual Health estimates that 3 percent to 5 percent of the U.S. population suffers from sexual compulsion disorders; however, this estimate only includes those actively seeking treatment for sexual addiction. There may be millions who are affected, living in the shadows, and not getting help.

Pornography, addiction, and cybersex are forms of sex addiction that have inexpensive and available gateways. Some indication of the extent of the problem is the amount of pornography available and used on the Internet. As of 2003, there were 1.3 million pornographic websites—260 million pages. Cybersex involves a noncontact sexual episode through private chats, either with or without a video connection. Seventy-six percent of victims in Internet-initiated sexual exploitation cases were 13 to 15 years old, and 75 percent were girls. "Most cases progressed to sexual encounters," according to the *Journal of Adolescent Health* (Dube et al. 2006), and 93 percent of the face-to-face meetings involved illegal or underage sex.

The difference between old-fashioned porn and Internet porn is a bit like the difference between wine and spirits. After hundreds of years as a mild intoxicant, erotica has undergone a sudden distillation. Digital porn is the equivalent of cheap gin in Georgian England: a reliable if unhygienic hit that relieves misery and boredom. And, unlike the old "dirty mags," it is available in limitless quantities" (Thompson 2012).

And cybersex appears to affect relationships. At a 2003 meeting of the American Academy of Matrimonial Lawyers, two-thirds of the 350 divorce lawyers who attended said that excessive interest in online porn played a significant role in the divorces of that year, where previously it had almost no role (Hagedorn 2009).

Sex Addiction that Begins in Childhood

Raymond's father is an alcoholic. His parents ran a funeral home and the family lived above it. Raymond was very much afraid of his father, who raged at him, and his mother and brother didn't offer much companionship, protection, or solace. An employee at the home, Caruso, took a shine to Raymond and spent time with him. He was big, gregarious, and paid attention to Raymond. Caruso often took Raymond to the basement to "train" him in the family business. His father approved. While initially this felt like much longed-for special attention, it eventually became an experience that sowed the seeds for a life-long pattern of sexual acting-out behaviors. In the course of "training," Caruso terrified Raymond by showing him dead bodies and body parts. He also exposed himself to Raymond and "he got me to do things to him." He told Raymond that if he told his parents what was going on, he would kill him. And Raymond, being a child and a frightened child at that, believed him. In Raymond's young mind, sex became fused with terror and abuse, a hand, a body, an erect penis. Sexual pleasure and sexual fear all became conflated in Raymond's mind.

It is no wonder that as an adult, Raymond himself became a womanizer and turned to alcohol and drugs to deal with the freaky imagery that he lived with and the state of anxiety his past left him with. He has had a string of careers; in his using days he was the owner of a strip club.

The longer the origins of Raymond's behavior went unaddressed, coupled with his use of drugs and alcohol as his "go to" for managing his pain, the more his sexual acting out escalated. Though some of the details of Raymond's story are unusual, the gist of this story I find all too common. There are many children in many basements "playing" or "being taken care of." The Raymond character carries terrible feelings of guilt and complicity. Though these victims were often very young at the time, say eight or so, the sexual liaison may have persisted over time, and they may have both feared and taken pleasure in it. They are left with the feeling that because they did not say no, they are somehow at fault. But trauma bonds make saying no extremely difficult, and the relationship described here between Raymond and Caruso is based on fear and subjugation; Caruso had the authority of age. He terrified Raymond and cut off any access to outside support that Raymond may have had by telling him that he would kill Raymond if he told; the more afraid Raymond was, the more he needed Caroso's "protection."

These same features can be part of a less obviously frightening situation if there is a power (age) imbalance, secrecy, and fear of being "found out" and a sense of one person being subjugated by the needs of the other. They are a recipe for a trauma bond.

Sex and Self-Soothing

We use sex for much more than reproduction. Orgasm releases dopamine into our bodies that makes us feel soothed, cared for, and alive. It is one of nature's great mood menders and bonders. But intense sexual stimulation, such as Internet pornography, can trigger a neurochemical high followed by a hangover or a withdrawal period. As dopamine drops, a sexual satiation neurochemical rises, and testosterone receptors decrease—all of which can radically affect mood for the worse or even bring on withdrawal symptoms. Some of this drop is natural, and if couples are lying in each other's arms, it can be a soothing and bonding time in which they can enjoy each other and affirm their affectionate feelings. If the drop is severe and a person is left feeling alone and perhaps disconnected, this withdrawal can feel like a letdown where emotions of shame or loneliness can make one want to do something to get rid of uncomfortable feelings, something that can spiral him or her further toward compulsivity.

Spending and Debting

We are a nation of consumers; buying is what keeps our economy afloat. Spending and debting are part of our landscape. Between 6 to 9 million people are estimated as affected by pathological gambling, which is now included in the *Diagnostic and Statistical Manual of Mental Disorders, Fourth Edition* (DSM-IV). Indeed, this seesawing between financial extremes has come back to haunt all of us from megacorporations to small households. Behaviors around money can fly out of balance through overspending, underspending, or a combination of the two. We can binge and purge with money just as with food; we can be financially sober, financially inebriated, or financially anorexic.

The Adrenaline-Endorphin High

Adrenaline, which the body releases when it is in a state of hyperarousal—the fight-or-flight response—rewards the body with a rush of exquisite pleasure and pain relief. When secreted into the bloodstream, it rapidly prepares the body for action. While some people get their adrenaline "fix" from driving too fast or skydiving, others get theirs from gambling, compulsive spending, overworking, or obsessive activity—all of which reflect problems with self-regulation and impulse control. Endorphins resemble opiates in their ability to produce a sense of well-being and are a natural pain killer. Both adrenaline and endorphins are part of the self-medicating cycle.

◊◊◊◊

Sandra and Dick came to a session with me as a couple; they were beginning to have some relationship issues. They had fallen madly in love at a conference and were married within three months. Dick was Sandra's fifth husband, and Sandra was Dick's third wife. As we explored what brought them to see me, it became obvious that Dick was very concerned about the way that Sandra spent money.

"About how much money did you spend, would you say?" I asked.

"Well, not that much really, around well, maybe thirty-five or forty-five thousand," Sandra answered sweetly.

"Which is it, do you think?" I asked, beginning to get a picture of her reluctance to acknowledge the amount.

"Well," said Sandra, without as much guilt as I might have expected, "maybe closer to forty-five thousand."

"How long did it take you to spend that amount?"

"I'm not sure, fifteen minutes maybe . . . maybe thirty," Sandra said sheepishly and with the look of a little girl who'd just eaten the first piece of someone else's birthday cake. She was acting like she had simply overspent a bit but that it was somehow not that big a deal.

"What did you buy that you spent that much so quickly?" I asked, imagining that it might be a piece of jewelry she'd been wanting.

"Oh, lots of things. I don't quite remember. A bracelet, I think, a lizard-skin jacket, some other stuff, some lingerie." She winked at her husband, who was now shifting his weight back and forth in his chair. The picture was beginning to take shape: a woman running frantically around a store, grabbing breathlessly at items she not only didn't particularly need, but ones she didn't even remember buying.

Dick chimed in, assuring me that he already had a plan in place to pay off this debt and that he would have it taken care of in, say, three years. Here is a couple who had been essentially out of control from day one, playing out their lack of relationship sobriety.

We might surmise that shopping engages Sandra in an adrenaline and or dopamine cycle. But when at home alone, sitting in a room with bags full of unnecessary purchases and no audience all that is left is a letdown—and a pile of unpaid bills and sometimes unattended relationships. Then a moment of panic at this self-created "emergency." The way for Sandra to feel better is to reengage in the self-medicating "relief" behavior.

The Wealth and Privilege Trap

Gary, who came with his family to a program where I was consulting, loves his work. Most of his waking hours are spent at the office or on an airplane, or recovering from those activities. He loves his family, too, who feel proud of his success and grateful for the money he earns and the many privileges that his success affords them.

Gary's wife, Katie, loves him. She finds herself, however,

increasingly attracted to her contractor who is so much a part of her life. It's so easy to talk things over with him. He's nice; he has fun, masculine energy; he's around. Katie feels guilty, but it's fun to fantasize about Frank. She misses her husband, but telling him that would do no good. He can't do anything about his long hours and all the travel. She wonders if he ever goes out when he travels.

Conner and Brooke, their children, wonder if there is a gap growing between their parents. They love them both: Mom's in charge, but when Dad comes home on weekends or for a vacation, they like spending time with him. But he seems so busy. So far away and so very wrapped up in what he does. Conner worries that he should do this kind of work, too, but at seventeen, he isn't sure he can see himself working like this or even wanting to. Besides, his dad is so successful, how could he ever get to wherever it is that his dad has gotten to? Conner would love to talk to his dad about all of this, but his dad seems so distracted when he is at home, like he carries the office around in his head even when he isn't there.

Katie sees Conner withdrawing from his dad but doesn't want to say anything to insinuate herself; after all, it's their relationship. And she doesn't want to think about how Gary is gone—these days, she's so used to it that she's not even sure how it would feel to have him around a lot. She is used to being in charge. Used to running things. It's simpler in a way. But lonely. Thank goodness she and Brooke are so close—she has a built-in friend. What a great daughter. Loads of friends, great grades. And Brooke is always so upbeat.

On weekends Katie and Gary go out with friends. Katie often

drinks a little too much these days. And now when Monday comes, well, why stop? Gary doesn't get home till so late that she barely sees him. She enjoys a glass or two of white wine while she is cooking dinner. And maybe one with dinner to sort of fill the evening and help her to relax with the kids. Sipping a glass as she falls asleep is soothing. Why not?

Sometimes Brooke feels like she is losing her best friend, but when she tries to talk to her dad about her mom's drinking, he doesn't do much. He says he'd deal with it, but Brooke isn't sure. And when she tries to talk to her mom about it, she doesn't get very far before her mom starts to complain about how much her dad works and tears up, and Brooke feels caught in the middle of two people she loves.

But Brooke and Conner have a lot of freedom and their parents are easy to get around, which isn't all that bad.

And Mom spends more time in her bedroom.

And Dad spends more time at the office and in front of the computer when he's at home.

And the house feels pretty empty, but Brooke and Conner can hang out downstairs with their friends or at the pool house and no one ever really bothers them. So it's cool, that way.

And their parents give them the credit card—money is just around.

This house is beautiful. Everyone who sees it thinks so. And Brooke and Conner seem so lucky. They have everything.

Conner discovers pot. He hides it, which isn't all that hard. *And so what*, Conner thinks, *Dad isn't around and Mom and Brooke have each other, and I don't want to work on Wall Street anyway.*

The Trap of Privilege

Children who grow up with privilege can feel confused by
their pain. They are, after all, so fortunate. And the world often
agrees with them. Their pain is somehow invisible, hidden
beneath a veneer of affluence, status, and all that comes with it.
Rich surroundings that look and feel full, nice clothes that allow
children of wealth to appear to have it together looking, even
though they may be falling apart on the inside, can deceive all
concerned, including the person in the mirror looking back at
his own elegant reflection. They feel deprived of something they
want but guilty about feeling it, because what do they have to
complain about?

But some of the factors that are part of a trauma-engendering
home can be exaggerated in affluent homes. The power imbalance can be greater. If parents are successful, it makes them taller
in the eyes of their child. And it sets the bar higher in the children's minds in terms of their own ability to eventually become
as big or bigger than their parent, which is every child's natural
wish. So there can be a sense of defeat, especially if the children
do not wish to identify with their parent or if their parent tends
toward narcissism and does not want anyone, including their
own children, to get as big as they are.

Next there is the trapped feeling. Children of wealth can iron-
ically have less access to outside support than their less advan-
taged counterparts. Their worlds tend to be circumscribed;
their privilege surrounds them and holds them in a narrow orbit
within which their parents may have an extended arm of control

and power. After all, what teacher really wants to confront a big, powerful person who carries the aura of prestige and success? Or is a major donor and pals around with school board members? This also holds true for other potential sources of outside support, like church, synagogue, tutors, or paid caretakers. And wealth can be isolating with its big houses and property. There is less need to be part of an interdependent community where dinners are family-oriented because it's easier and cheaper not to get a babysitter and kids get dragged along on parents' errands or stay with a neighbor or friend. Children with less privilege may paradoxically have more spontaneous freedom, less isolation, and less loneliness.

When families such as these are also alcoholic, they have much to lose by letting the cat out of the bag and may go to great lengths to hide the disease of addiction from their communities and even from themselves. And they can afford it. The addict's bottom can be very low because the family can financially afford to "sponsor" their use. If the main wage earner is the nonaddict, the using can go on indefinitely because there may be no financial consequences. With privilege goes expectation. Wealthy families are often "looking-good" families; so are many types of successful families at all levels of the social and economic scale. Religious and military families, for example, can have very stringent standards, and can trap children in a similar manner if they put rules above personal needs and looking good above being good..

Additionally, being the child of someone whose primary focus in life is that of attaining wealth and/or status can be a disillusioning and disheartening experience. The family wealth or status can become a primary source of identity which family members develop a deep dependency. If we grow up with wealth from childhood, that dependency is wrapped around each stage of development. Money can be a great drug, a mood manager, a high. Separating the person from the identity as someone of wealth, privilege, and perceived (and often real) power can be like separating the person from their substance. Children of privilege can despair at ever doing anything that will match the success of the wealth-getter, and the wealth-getter may well only value those sorts of pursuits that lead to amassing wealth.

From Compulsivity to Balance

The desire to manage compulsive behaviors or an inner world that is out of balance reflects a self-affirming step toward personal growth and greater self-awareness. It is important that we understand that these behaviors developed slowly and over time. And that some of the issues that we are avoiding or self-medicating may have begun as far back as our childhoods. It is equally important to understand that our solutions will be slow and require long-term commitment, and to understand that commitment itself will become its own reward—developing each day in us a little more patience, self-awareness, self-love, acceptance, and comfort living in our own skin.

Once we understand that self-medication is an unconscious attempt to manipulate our own body chemistry to feel more pleasure and less pain, to keep our own foot on the "dose delivery" pedal, we can flip it on its head. We can learn to manipulate our body chemistry in self-constructive—rather than self-destructive—ways.

PART IV:

Healing the ACoA Trauma Syndrome

The Lord is my shepherd; I shall not want.
He maketh me to lie down in green pastures:
he leadeth me beside the still waters.
He restoreth my soul: he leadeth me
in the paths of righteousness for his name's sake.
Yea, though I walk through the valley of the shadow of death,
I will fear no evil: for thou art with me;
thy rod and thy staff they comfort me.
Thou prepares a table before me in the presence of mine enemies: thou
anointest my head with oil; my cup runneth over.
Surely goodness and mercy shall follow me all the days of my life:
and I will dwell in the house of the Lord forever.

—King James Version

TWELVE

Recovering from the ACoA Trauma Syndrome: Reclaiming the Disowned Self

Some people's lives seem to flow in a narrative; mine
had many stops and starts. That's what trauma does. It
interrupts the plot. You can't process it because it doesn't fit
with what came before or what comes afterward. A friend of
mine, a soldier, put it this way. In most of our lives, most of the
time, you have a sense of what is to come. There is a steady
narrative, a feeling of "lights, camera, action" when big events
are imminent. But trauma isn't like that. It just happens, and
then life goes on. No one prepares you for it.

—Jessica Stern, *Denial: A Moment of Terror*

Change is not only intellectual. When it comes to trauma, we need to create a new body to live in. We need to learn to take good care of it so that it stays healthy and emotionally fit. We need to resolve the kind of hidden pain that locks us into triggered, knee-jerk reactions that, once set into motion, have a life of their own. Change comes when we have sat in the pain long enough and fully enough so that we can feel it, can open our mouths and talk about it, see it for what it is, reorder and understand it, and then walk out of it. This does not mean that we won't feel bad, hurt, angry, or triggered about our past again. It just means that if and when we are triggered, we won't catapult into an unconscious place from which we can only act out, shut down, or dive straight into self-medicating behaviors.

Eventually, our "triggered place" will feel somehow less compelling, less like "all" of us, less like we want to give it so much (or so suspiciously little) of our attention. Change occurs when we have a choice about whether or not we care to direct our attention toward or away from what is being triggered, when our triggers no longer run us, and when we're able to manage the feelings that they bring up with our own skills, when our spontaneous reaction to a situation that used to baffle us changes (Moreno 1953). Change also comes when we learn to do something different, to make choices in our thinking and daily routines that interrupt a downward spiral and create an upward one.

We heal one feeling at a time, one thought at a time. As each feeling arises, we unpack it and look at the thinking, meaning-making, and behavior it gives rise to; we give the feelings air, voice, and freedom of expression. We make new, mature sense of them with our adult mind. We learn from them, and we grow up on the inside. Emotional maturity rather than an act of will is, in this sense, a natural outgrowth of deep work—an awakening into another point of view and a letting go of the past in order to live more fully in the present (T. Dayton 2007).

The ACoA trauma syndrome is baked into the psyche of the CoA during crucial periods of child development, which is why healing takes time. It's a peeling back the layers of the onion one at a time, stage by stage, examining the thinking, feeling, and behavior that were learned and became engrained at each stage of development. Physical sobriety is fairly straightforward, and abstention or regulation are its mainstays, but emotional sobriety can be more elusive.

Why Experiential Forms of Therapy Are Necessary for Healing Trauma

Talk alone does not reach the parts of the brain that process trauma (van der Kolk 1994). Healing trauma requires a combination of therapy and lifestyle changes. Because emotional and sensory memory are processed by and stored in the body, the most successful forms of therapy for trauma are experiential. Experiential forms of therapy and therapy "supports" like journaling, exercise, guided imagery, walking, yoga, and breathing have been finding their way into treatment programs for decades because they work. Psychodrama—a role playing/experiential method of therapy—has become a therapy of choice in addressing the mind/body issues of trauma. Experiential therapy and psychodrama can allow us to bring emotions that may be in some way numb or hard to access toward a conscious level where we can hopefully feel, unfreeze, and talk about them.

One of the problems with shutting down feeling is that we

begin to live in our heads. We tell ourselves a story about what we *think* we're feeling or what we think we *should* be feeling rather than *feeling* our genuine emotions and allowing words to grow out of them so we can accurately describe our inner experience. When we can feel our feelings and then translate them into language, we can use our reasoning ability to play a role in regulating our emotional experience.

Trauma can leave us feeling shattered inside. Valuable pieces of ourselves are frozen, hidden from view, or split off from our conscious awareness and have not been adequately integrated into our working model of our "selves." Dealing with, giving voice and movement to those shards of self that hold valuable feeling and sensory memories, so that they can be reseen, reinterpreted, and reintegrated into the adult self with mature understanding and reasoning attached to them, allows us to feel whole again and to better understand ourselves.

Creative arts approaches to healing, like writing, psychodrama, sociometry, music, and guided imagery, allow the traumatized mind to find a voice in a nonthreatening way. They include right-brain processes. The right brain envisions the whole; it synthesizes the big picture so that the trauma story can emerge in a different kind of voice. I have incorporated all of these approaches in my model *Relationship Trauma Repair* (relationshiptraumarepair. com), which is in use in treatment centers, clinics, and private practices around the country. The model's group exercises offer hundreds of tiny moments in which clients can warm up to their own story, translate feelings into words, share them, and then reach out and connect with others in the same emotional boat. It uses journaling and guided imagery to teach skills of emotional processing, emotional literacy, and self-regulation. I have also designed a creative arts self-help website (visit www.emotionexplorer.com) that offers users may of these approaches online.

Therapy for ACoAs needs to involve processes that allow us to warm up to frozen feelings in relative safety and *then* talk about them. ACoAs need to feel, then speak. When we say "tell me about your trauma," we may be putting someone who has been traumatized in the humiliating and embarrassing position of feeling emotionally stupid. Some may be able to talk with feeling and fluidity, having not blocked their own feelings, others, who have less concious awareness of what might be stored within them, might either give it their.best guess, sign on to the therapist's version of what happened, read as if from a script of symptoms, or stare at their therapist and say, "Well," and (unfortunately all too often), "Let me think about it."

Healing from Sexual Abuse

When Kathy came to our group, you might say she "lived in her head." The kinds of body/mind memories and flashbacks of childhood abuse that haunted her were so disturbing that she just didn't want have to feel and remember them. But they plagued her nonetheless. Their constant, gnawing presence within her made her feel different and not a part of the group. She worried that group members would find her story sickening. She always looked a bit startled and on guard. She struggled with feeling like an underachiever, with organizing herself, with poor self-care and overeating. About a year into our group, Kathy began to feel comfortable enough to let her story come out.

The following psychodrama is of severe sexual abuse. I include it because it clearly illustrates how much can be repaired through role-play. The story is in Kathy's own voice; she now wants to tell her story because she has had enough of hiding it.

> *The only time he allowed me to open my mouth was when he wanted to put his gigantic penis in it. Gigantic because I was three and my father was a grown man, six feet, four inches tall. I'm not sure what the smile on his face was about: having an orgasm or suffocating me as close to death as he could. When he wasn't doing that, he was screaming at me that I had ruined his life and he would kill me . . . he said when I was sleeping he would come and kill me. Those things made him feel so much better; that's how it looked to me, anyway. They made me freeze and disappear and be afraid to let people know that I was alive.*

I think it is important to understand that for at least a year, all Kathy did was comment on other people's psychodramas, often giving well-thought-through commentary and congratulations that often sounded somewhat removed from the emotion of the moment. It took her a long time to trust the group and herself. Initially, she gave us the facts but without much feeling. For some time, Kathy said it was enough "work" just to sit in group and tolerate being around the intense emotion sometimes expressed and the feelings, or lack of feeling, that she became aware of in herself. She bonded and trusted a little more each week, hesitant but very sincere. She had a long pattern of dissociation from her abuse, so just coming back into her body and mind was a challenge. She could remain physically present, but her consciousness was somewhere else.

When sharing, she might say something like, "I just feel so . . . I just . . . he . . . and I couldn't." Small tears and withheld sobs would work their way toward the surface and then disappear. Kathy would bring her hand to her chest and throat as she tried to breathe and speak. I would ask questions like, "If your throat could talk, what would it want to say? What would your hand like to do?"

"I don't know. Go away? Get away? Get off me? Push?" Then muffled sobs, then quiet, then nothing.

This sort of narrating happened many times. For a while, I just made use of opportunities to draw out another sentence or two. As Kathy began to speak more about her abuse, she had some sensations of choking and not being able to breathe, along with a combination of helplessness and burning rage. These feelings remained unexpressed, though she became increasingly aware of how they felt inside of her (she later described them as tingly, shaky, queasy, blocked, and shivers). Kathy became more able to allow herself to experience and articulate her feelings rather than shut them down. She regularly experienced feelings of being trapped beneath her father's weight and having her breathing choked off. Her body was recalling the experience it had recorded, and in doing so, the sensations that accompanied the scenes of abuse emerged as well. The words were at first tentative, few, and far between. But she got a tremendous amount from other people's work; it felt safer to watch and learn rather than to enter into her own role-play. This is the beauty of psychodrama: you can heal in and from every role whether that of "group member," auxiliary role player (playing a role in another person's drama) or protagonist (the person whose story is being role played).

Kathy talked about what she learned from someone whose story provided a link into her own:

> *Sally has been in group longer than I have and also has "father issues." She taught me how to scream. It was one of the most beautiful sounds I have ever heard. She could scream so loud at her father . . . with hate and rage. I loved coming to group and hearing Sally scream at the top of her lungs, and now I can do it, too . . . even while beating the crap out of him with a bataka (foam bat). I always feel lighter and freer after one of those sessions. Recently, wanting more freedom from my "death sentence" so that I can live life more fully, I got to beat the crap out of him again, while yelling NO! What a gift. Another glorious feeling.*

Kathy literally felt that she would die of her father's abuse, for obvious reasons; she could barely breath when it was occurring. Simply shouting "no" over and over again allowed Kathy to move away from her collapsed, helpless position toward the emancipation of outrage, which was the appropriate and natural response to being subjugated by her father. Because psychodrama is experiential, we can bring the body into the work. In the case of sexual or physical abuse, it can help to allow the protagonist to feel they are fighting back, successfully defending themselves or really expressing their stored rage and helplessness, to take the reempowering actions that they never got a chance to take, to stand up straight and fight back. Experiential expression of rage is always done in safety, using only a bataka and a tackle dummy. This kind of rage, if not expressed in therapy, can easily leak out in other ways; therapy allows us to become conscious of how much of it we may be carrying. But rage is by no means the whole story; beneath it is often helplessness, collapse, sadness, confusion, distorted bonding, yearning, and so forth. The rage needs to be experienced in a context and the full flush of feelings, mentations, and actions explored.

In a traumatic moment, children may not have had the opportunity to discharge the adrenaline of the flight response if they were outpowered by a drunk or abusive parent. Their freeze response is stored in their bodies. As feelings and memories return, so does their urge to shake, move, run, or take defensive action. Kathy wanted to shake off the "energy, prickles, and tensions" inside of her, and she did—over and over again. We did a combination of talking about what happened, participating in the work of others, empty chair work, and psychodrama role-plays to work with Kathy's abuse. Her work spanned about three years before this next drama occurred.

After talking to her father in a role-play and raging at him (which she had already done a few times), I asked her what she would like to do next. "Today he would be sent to jail for what he did to me. I want him to be sent to jail," was Kathy's firm response. The beauty of psychodrama is that a scene like this, so appropriate as a part of retribution, can actually be structured and played out. Kathy chose group members who arrested her father and "took him to court" for his crimes against her.

> *I was in charge of the sentencing. At first, I thought I'd sentence him to death. But then, as a big smile came on me, I realized what would give him the most pain. Torture even. So I sentenced him to silence. He could never utter another word. My father, the narcissist, who demanded that everyone listen to him, could never say another word. I was in heaven. And then the jailor took my father to prison. I stood there, drinking in the picture; heaven doesn't begin to describe my feeling at that moment.*

This is the kind of retribution for being hurt that people seek in life that can get them into trouble. Psychodrama allows them to seek it therapeutically. One way trauma becomes intergenerational when we reverse roles with our abusers and pass pain down unconsciously—when we, in a sense, become them. Psychodrama allows the abused person to gain conscious retribution so that both their pain and their need to act out their pain is done consciously and in service of healing rather than unconsciously.

Kathy walked around freely repeating variations of "you are never to speak again, the court has sentenced you." Her ability to put her father away from her and to actually "see" him locked up and punished was deeply relieving to her. She could see and record a picture of her father behind bars and feel safe from her memories, safe from the nightmares that he could still find her and come into her bedroom. It also reduced the intensity and frequency of her intrusive memories, significantly lessened her hypervigilance, and allowed her to feel supported, protected, and cared about by other group members. Kathy was unable to get away when she was a child, but now she could get away and take back her authority; she could empower herself.

Kathy continued:

> When it was over and it was time for people to "de-role" and process, I looked out onto the group of people who were sitting in the room. In that moment I heard person after person tell me what a horrible thing my father had done to me. Many were angry, upset, and a few wanted to kill him on my behalf. It was glorious.
>
> I am blessed to be surrounded by people who I trust and who "have my back." And, for the first time, I felt like I was out of jail. The experience of my secret horror being witnessed and validated gave me a sense of freedom I had never felt before. It also gave me another first: the ability to recognize and feel the courage and bravery that I had heard so many people speak about after I would work. I could now give myself the "standing ovation" that I deserved by surviving and, thanks, to psychodrama, I could now use that courage to go beyond surviving to the living part.

Kathy speaks here both to the power of letting the body not only "tell" but "show" or express its story. And her story speaks to the value of compassionate witnessing. It is remarkable what giving someone the "stage" on which to *show* his or her story can do for someone.

As a child, Kathy had been completely disempowered. She felt she had no one to go to for comfort or protection. She experienced her father as having the authority to subjugate her to his needs

and she could not "tell." She felt also that she had no part in deciding what was going to happen to her, let alone any influence over
her father's feelings. We reversed this pattern in psychodrama. We
allowed Kathy to "lead the way." She was the person structuring
scene after scene, deciding who she wished to talk to and when
that would happen. She was able to mobilize the resources available to her in the room by showing her story, choosing people to
help her by playing roles, allow others to witness her story, and
take in their support. And finally, she was the one handing out
punishment to her father with the help of her "community." The
child within her, who naturally wished for some form of revenge
or retribution, had her day in court. If she could not completely
replace the old experience, her new one could slide in beside it.
She could finally separate past from present by psychodramati-
cally redressing a wrong that had been done to her.

Dealing with Dissociation and Frozenness

Our frozen fragments of self can hold much information
about what drives us—they whisper to our inner ear about who
we are or who we aren't. While Kathy's experience is extreme,
sexual abuse is not uncommon when alcohol and drugs reduce
inhibitions and drive behavior. Sexual abuse, in its many forms,
can contribute to dissociation and lack of physical and/or emotional expression. By processing these fragments of self, we make
significant moves toward integration. Pieces of the puzzle begin
to fall together and we feel more empowered, whole, and self-

aware. Because Kathy has frightening "sense memories" and relationship moments or dynamics woven into her memories of her father, she can get thrown back into a frozen and dissociated state when she feels triggered by intimacy, sex, or even closeness. What triggers each of us is uniquely individual. But for ACoAs, it is often something that returns us to that childhood state of feeling trapped, vulnerable, helpless, humiliated, scared, minimized, or less than. "If you do not discharge the freeze response, you loose resiliency and the ability to face further threat" (Scaer 2007). While Kathy's example is extreme, being repeatedly raged at or at the whim of a drunk parent and told we are the problem, or being unprotected by the sober parent, can also be traumatizing over time.

Dissociation remains the bête noire *of psychiatric diagnoses. Its features include . . . a disruption in the usually integrated functions of consciousness, memory, or perception of the environment* (DSM-IV 477), *but a unitary diagnosis continues to evade us. We refer to states of depersonalization, derealization, distorted time and sensory perception, fugue states, amnesia and dissociative identity disorder. . . . But psychotherapy practitioners in the field know full well what dissociation is. It's that confused, distracted state in your patient that prevents you from breaking through the fog into any semblance of meaningful contact. It's the patient "leaving the room," losing contact with you when you've barely touched on the meaningful traumatic material, or when an obtuse reference to some supposedly benign topic causes a short circuit to a traumatic cue in their memory. . . . It's that state of detachment . . . regardless of technique or therapist* (Scaer 2012).

When Kathy entered group, she had just been fired for the third consecutive time. Though she is very talented in her work, she went blank when confronted with paperwork, and she felt too intimidated by her various employers, too disempowered and frozen within herself, to ask for help. After all, asking for help when she was young was not possible; that got her nowhere at best and abused at worst. Those core beliefs, that opening her mouth and speaking up would lead to trouble and that no one could help her, had lasted through adulthood. When Kathy could not manage an important part of her job, it triggered her back into the helplessness, choicelessness, and immobility she felt as a child. And she could not take action to improve her situation. She dissociated and disappeared into what felt like nowhere, but was not nowhere at all: it was somewhere, and that somewhere was associated with her traumatic experiences with her father, an authority figure in her life. When she bumped up against the authority of a boss, a system, and a workplace, her past become triggered. When she could not manage the task in front of her, she froze; she became unable to take action on her own behalf, just as when she was young. Instead, she went into a place of feeling totally overwhelmed. Gradually working through her "frozen feelings", reestablishing a sense of autonomy, freedom of movement, and choice allowed her to literally "create new memories," ones in which she was a functioning, empowered adult able to both enjoy her life in the present and muster the resilience to meet continued life challenges. Kathy has now been at her current job for three years and is very happy, effective, and valued.

THIRTEEN

Resilience: Mobilizing Help and Support

Your time is limited, so don't waste it living someone else's life.
Don't be trapped by dogma—which is living with the results
of other people's thinking. Don't let the noise of other's opinions
drown out your own inner voice. And most important, have
the courage to follow your heart and intuition. They somehow
already know what you truly want to become.

—Steve Jobs

While it is indeed critical to go back and rework significant issues that block our ability to be present in the here and now, focusing exclusively on the negative qualities of ourselves, others, and the damage they wreak on our lives can sometimes have the adverse effect of weakening the self and our relationships rather than strengthening them. Nothing is black and white, and no one—not even the most fortunate among us— makes it through life unscathed. So what questions do we need to ask ourselves in order to find that invisible line between too little and too much focus on a painful past? Is there some sort of magical number of adverse events or circumstances that become too many to overcome, or can they be offset by positive events or the way in which we handle the difficult cards that life deals us? If the latter, what are the determining factors? Following are some of the most common questions that I see clinicians and those in recovery grappling with:

- What factors actually do go into creating what we call resilience?
- Why are some people able to meet adversity and overcome it or even grow from it while others seem more disabled by it?
- Is there a healthy version of "psychological defenses" like repression, denial, intellectualization, or minimization that allows us to move forward and cope?
- Is there such a thing as too much therapy or self-reflection?
- How can I build and sustain strength and resilience?

Resilience is a dynamic and interactive process that builds on itself; it is not just a state of self but of self in relationship. The ability of the child to access friends, mentors, and community supports is a significant part of what allows one child to do well where another might experience a tougher time. Resilient kids tend to have "protective factors" that buffer bad breaks. In studies of children, two of those resilience-enhancing factors that have emerged time and again are good cognitive functioning (like cognitive self-regulation and basic intelligence) and positive relationships (especially with competent adults, like parents or grandparents). Children who have protective factors in their lives tend to do better in some challenging environments when compared with children, in the same environments, without protective factors (Yates et al 2003; Luthar 2006).

Resilient children are able to adapt when they encounter adversity or stress and use their support system to their advantage; they soak up positive feelings from their environment "surreptitiously," incorporate them, and use them to their advantage (Wolin and Wolin 1993). A kind neighbor, a grandparent or relative, a faith-based institution, or an unchaotic school environment, along with a child's ability to make positive use of them, are formative to resilience. Terrible things happen to people all over the world, but interwoven with those terrible things are often the meaningful sources of support that help people to overcome their circumstances and go on to have purposeful and meaningful lives. In working through the pain of a traumatic past, it is important to help clients to identify not only what hurt them, but what sustained them.

Take Annette, for example. Her father is a lawyer and her mother has a successful career in marketing. She lives on Manhattan's Upper East Side and attended a private girls' school; she lives in a world of financial and social privilege.

At the age of ten and a half, when her parents decided to split up, Annette says that she "brokered a deal" with her parents that she would live with her dad if he promised to stop pressuring her mom for her sister to live with him, too. After the separation, her mother and sister moved to northern California. She saw her mother one week per year and her sister for two.

I am a perfectionist. I just try to get everything so right and I am exhausted. I do well in my work but I work so hard, I dot every "I" and cross every "t" and then do it all over again. I love what I do but it's using me up. I feel depleted. I think I am a workaholic; [work] is where I feel good about myself, but I can't work like this anymore. I am always available to everyone, all the time, that's why they like me, I never say no. My last consulting lasted four years and now I am taking a leave of absence. But I feel depressed.

I say I want to get in touch with my feelings and acknowledge the fear and sadness coming from my heart, but when it comes down to it, I am too terrified to sit in dialog with all that I have successfully stuffed down since I was 11.

Though Annette experienced a high level of trauma as a child, she was also able to make use of and mobilize the supports at her disposal. She is a classic example of having used them to her advantage. She has grown up to have a successful career in human rights and a committed, loving relationship with a partner, but she suffers with stress-related physical ailments and depression. Her awareness of her issues and her wish to deal with them are resilient qualities. Annette works with the international business community on ensuring that human (including child) rights, labor rights, environmental protection, and anticorruption standards are maintained. She has, in a sense, been able to stand up for herself in proxy; having had her own human rights trampled over, she has fought for others, for children, and gained a powerful sense of mission and meaning. Her interest clearly grew out of her childhood.

My greatest passion was for other cultures, and one of my earliest memories is asking my parents to wake me up at 5 AM on a regular basis when I was five to watch a show on TV about Africa. They thought I was nuts since they have no interest in other countries, but they were okay with it. I also took Swahili at the local public library and an African cooking class for kids when I was six. I also asked my teacher in third grade if I could be the official welcome guide for foreign students joining our class. We only had one person from another country join the class over the years, but the experience of learning about her culture and helping her integrate made me feel very fulfilled. When I was fifteen, I went on teen tours to different countries, and the experiences fueled my interest in cross-cultural relations.

Though she is from a Protestant religious background, her family did not attend church, which is, for many children, a source of support, values, and community.

My parents were, sadly, neither religious nor spiritual. We did not go to any house of worship, and the only gods we prayed to were Santa at Christmas and the Easter Bunny on Easter. I was envious of friends who did belong to a religious community as the congregation seemed like an exten- sion of family who looked out for their well-being. As an adult, while I am spiritual and self-identify as a Buddhist, I have yet to relinquish control of my life to a Divine Presence. Instead, I live life vigilantly—substituting faith for living on constant alert, with an arsenal of goal-orientation, will-power, and dogged determination at the ready to deploy at any time. I feel life will work out if I work hard enough to keep it safe. This means performing at inhuman standards that can rarely be met.

A week ago, we did a psychodrama with Rick, an actor who has been in recovery from his ACoA issues and cigarette smoking. Rick's work, as with any actor, is intermittent; he was in a dry period and feeling depressed. Annette participated for only a few minutes in Rick's drama, but I was not surprised when I received these journal entries. She was both dotting every "I" and crossing every "t" and in typically resilient fashion, "soaking up" healing and recovery wherever there was an opportunity she could make use of.

> When I was asked to play Rick's stand-in, kneeling down on the stage, I felt what stagnation and depression looked like, and it convinced me that I have been struggling with depression on and off for six months—since the end of my last consultancy. It seems no "co-inky-dink" that the depression set in when the working ceased. It is my distraction, my drug, my self-soothing . . . and provides me with self-esteem and validation that I am not worthless.

In this manner, Annette was very appropriately making use of the ways in which she identified with Rick's drama as she was absorbing her own learning, while still playing the role as requested. Her journaling continued:

> I am really struggling to arrive at a good balance, but it is tough since the work that I do generally means I need to be composed and have enough self-esteem to lead and act as an authority, and I can't do that while having a dialog with my heart about the terror of childhood—let alone feel the terror. I guess I need to get more skillful compartmental-

izing—switching between functioning in the present and processing the past—but it is tough and I am not at all sure I can switch between "leader" mode and "okay, let me lose my shit and feel all that I stuffed in for thirty years" mode well enough to do either well. As someone who suffers with perfectionism, not doing either professional work or recovery well creates a whole new set of issues that I am all too ready to beat myself up about.

Annette has really put her own finger on her own issues. This is the beauty of psychodrama: in the process of breaking out—concretizing and experiencing life roles—we get clearer on what might be going onside inside of us. This can happen just as successfully whether it is our own drama or we are simply witnessing or playing a role in someone else's drama. In fact, where trauma is concerned, sometimes we can see more clearly if it is not our own role-play.

From here on, some of the heartbreaking details of Annette's story begin to emerge. Annette's father was a functional alcoholic, who she feels was probably self-medicating an undiagnosed psychiatric disorder. He was violent, sexually abusive, and clearly mood-disordered. He was also very focused on Annette; she says he was "devoted" to her but the devotion was both sincere and sick. It became a very confusing and painful legacy for Annette to untangle.

My dad often put pressure on me to sleep in his bed rather than in my own room. My housekeeper seemed surprised and concerned when she came in the mornings to see my bed not slept in. This happened often. I remember waking up on my dad's side of the bed on my back with his hands on my breasts and his face close to mine. I never sleep on my back, so it is odd to sleep in this position. This happened often. I would ask, "What are you doing?" He would say, "Just tucking you in." I would say, "I don't want to be tucked in." Then I would drift off again or get away to my room, but I think most of the time I drifted off again because I couldn't get up even though I did not want to be there. I was very tired; it was like waking out of a deep sleep—that quality of heavy sleep.

My dad walked around the house nude when I was eleven to sixteen, and when I complained, he invited me to do the same. I have dreams about my dad and me in bed in a sexual act, and I feel this awful feeling of shame.

Annette is not sure if what she dreamed actually happened or not, but clearly her level of abuse was trauma-inducing and stole her sense of autonomy over her body and parts of herself. But nothing is simple; she also felt loved by her father and he gave her a sense of being a special and capable human being. Children have many different experiences with their parents, and one of the things that makes being abused by a parent so potentially trauma-inducing is that the same person who you love, who is making you feel good about yourself, is the one abusing you and inducing feelings of pain and shame.

To my dad's credit, he always told me I was smarter than him and worked harder, so if I put my mind to it, I could do anything I wanted to do as long as I applied myself. So this gave me a sense of confidence and being able to accomplish anything I set my heart to doing, regardless of the obstacles that stood in my way.

I asked Annette if she had mentors who helped her in some way.

> *Mostly I had "idols" rather than mentors and spent much of my lonely preteen years trying to reach out to them and be acknowledged. In retrospect, they were a rather sad array of Hollywood and Broadway "stars" ranging from a smart, entrepreneurial woman actor to a comedian who was a "goodie-goodie," made people smile, and diffused discomfort with silly jokes. When I became old enough to expose myself to other cultures and value systems, I chose Gandhi and Thich Nhat Hahn as mentors, as well as various people who lead social justice movements in solidarity with marginalized communities in developing countries.*

I often see this with ACoAs; they soak up models from all sorts of sources to help them get pictures of who or how they might someday be. Trauma can affect a person's ability to envision a future; it may be that by looking toward stars in the firmament, children are able to picture themselves in a life beyond their circumstances.

Recovery from trauma involves "remembering" traumatic moments and circumstances and processing them. But it also needs to involve remembering the protective factors that got us through. In the same way that resilient kids mobilized these "helpers" in childhood, we need to mobilize our memories of these "helpers" as adults so that we can make use of them mentally and emotionally as sustaining inner resources. I continued to ask Annette if she remembered any "protective relationships" that helped along the way.

My housekeeper's presence gave me a lot of solace. She was a large, warm African-American woman who filled the house with a nice mama-like energy. Often she made cookies and meals. I pretended she was my mom. The only sad part was she left at four every afternoon to go home to be a mama to her own child. I think she knew that there was hushed violence in the home, and when she was there, I felt safe because my dad did not rage around her, most likely because she left at about the same time he came home from work, but nonetheless, in my mind, she gave me protection.

I asked if she had any friends whose families provided comfort.

I had close friends and their families and tried to spend time in their homes since they were not often allowed in mine. This time provided me with a safe haven and exposed me to different cultures where I felt much more at home. The time spent with a diplomatic family and a royal family nourished my interest in diplomacy and cross-cultural relations. Also, the doorman in my building often was asked by neighbors to call up on the intercom and ensure that everything was okay during my father's fits of violence. My dad would immediately answer in a calm voice, so no one ever intervened, but the presence of the doorman and the knowledge that he could potentially call up when things got bad gave me a sense of protection.

It is clear that her "protectors" gave Annette some sense that what was going on with her father was somehow not right. It is touching to realize how much it can mean to a child in need to feel that someone in their immediate world has an eye out for them.

"Was school a supportive community?" I asked.

It was supportive academically and in terms of fostering my artistic endeavors, but not in terms of intervening in the manner in which my dad raised me. A few teachers did show concern from time to time, but never to the point of intervention. My art teacher took an interest in my work and seemed to see that I was using mixed media to process pain. She gave me a lot of support to continue to tap my creative spirit and even took my father aside once to tell him that I was very talented and that it would be good for him to allow me to pursue my interest in art rather than being coerced to play the team sports that he excelled at.

I think my imagination and the fantasy life I expressed through art (painting and mixed media) provided me with protection from reality and gave me a socially acceptable way to process pain, fear, and grief while receiving positive attention for my work. It was a discrete way to tell people what was going on.

A creative outlet can be enormously helpful to a child who cannot put what she is going through into words. Children think in imagery. It is useful here to note that for the child at risk, it may be the kinds of indirect interventions from housekeepers, friends, parents, doormen, and art teachers—people who touch the life of the child directly and daily—that make the critical difference.

Annette also made great use of extracurricular activities that are so helpful to all children. For the child at risk, outside interests and after-school programs serve the purpose of keeping them out of the house and giving alternative sources of friendship, support, community, and self-esteem.

I always had a very strong interest in social work and social justice and was the head of the Social Service Committee at my school for a few years. We did outreach work in the community and it was natural for me to lead these efforts. Additionally, I was a gifted swimmer and always the captain of the swim team. It was rare for me to lose a race, so I developed a lot of self-confidence and leadership qualities. At one point, I was recruited for a pre-Olympic training camp, but I chose to stay in New York rather than move to Florida to train since I wanted to spend my time doing arts and academics rather than swimming twenty-four hours a day.

Therapists and researchers Steven Wolin, MD, and Sybil Wolin, PhD, observe in their book *The Resilient Self* that resilience seems to develop out of the challenge to maintain self-esteem. Troubled families often make their children feel powerless and bad about themselves. But resilient children find ways to feel good about themselves and life in spite of the powerful influence of their parents. Understanding these resilient qualities and how they develop helps to counter what the Wolins refer to as the "damage" model—the idea that if you've had a troubled childhood, you are condemned to a troubled adulthood or you are operating without strengths. In fact, resilience helps us to acknowledge that adversity can actually develop strength.

Personal Qualities of Resilience

In their research on ACoAs, the Wolins identified some of the following factors as contributing to ACoAs who were able to live successful lives in spite of any deficits they may have grown up with. They found that resilient people tended to:

- Find and build on their own strengths.
- Improve deliberately and methodically on their parents' life-styles.
- Marry consciously into happy, healthy, and/or strong families.
- Fight off memories of horrible family get-togethers and create new, more satisfying holidays and rituals.
- Live at least at a "magic two-hundred mile" radius from their families of origin, enabling them to be connected but somewhat apart from the daily fray of potential family dysfunction (1993).

Wolin and Wolin found that the liabilities of resilience tended to be physical/health related issues and relationship issues. Their research also revealed a number of personality and behavioral characteristics shared by resilient adults who moved through early family trauma and became thriving, successful adults:

- They can *talk* about and share their problems with those willing to listen or who may be able to lend a helping hand.
- They can be wonderfully *creative;* for many, creativity was a way to meet their own needs, or to make sense of, express, or even escape from what was going on around them.
- Graveyard *humor,* as any ACoA or addict can show you, often gets honed to a fine art as a coping skill. Thus, this can be a very funny population.

- Children from troubled homes often become very *independent* from a young age because they learn that they cannot necessarily depend upon their parents.
- The ones who thrive often do so because they have exercised *initiative* and have taken the reins into their own hands, recognizing that if they didn't do it, no one would or perhaps could.
- Oftentimes *morality* is developed as much from seeing what should not be done as what should. Those who have been wounded can have clear life lessons on what hurts and may feel determined not to hurt others in similar ways. They may even become altruistic, dedicating parts of their own lives to helping others.
- The *inventiveness* of those who have thrived in spite of the odds can be quite remarkable in dealing with problems. Because they have had to "think outside the box" to solve complex family situations, these thrivers can be highly creative and original, which are real assets both at home and in the workplace.
- This group has also had to develop *courage* and *grit*. They don't expect to be handed things and have long ago absorbed the reality that we don't always get what we want in life and that life isn't always fair. Indeed, those who grew up with emotional trauma can sometimes be quite dogged, working hard even if the rewards are not always forthcoming.

One of the cardinal findings of virtually all research on resilience is that those who thrived had at least one secure bonded relationship, usually within the family system.

Researchers like Emmy Werner and Ruth Smith, who conducted the famous long-term studies in Kauai, Hawaii, on resilient children, and Steve and Sybil Wolin, who studied resilience in children who grew up specifically with addiction, provide some valuable insights and answers about the general characteristics of the resilient children they observed (Wolin and Wolin 1993, 1995; Werner 1992; Werner and Smith 2001).

- They had likable personalities from birth that attracted parents, surrogates, and mentors to want to care for them. They were naturally adept recruiters of support and interest from others and drank up attention and care from wherever they could get it.
- They tended to be of at least average intelligence, reading on or above grade level.
- Few had another sibling born within two years of their birth.
- Virtually all of the children had at least one person with whom they had developed a strong relationship, often from the extended family or a close community member.
- Often they report having an inborn feeling that their lives were going to work out.

As adults this group shows the following qualities.

- They can identify the illness in their family and are able to find ways to distance themselves from it; they don't let the family dysfunction destroy them.

- They work through their problems but don't tend to make that a lifestyle.
- They take active responsibility for creating their own successful lives.
- They tend to have constructive attitudes toward themselves and their lives.
- They tend not to fall into self-destructive lifestyles.

Faith Based Communities: Spirituality, Strength, and Doggedness

Faith-based institutions can be a nourishing and character-building experience for children. They provide community, values, stability, and safe haven if they are healthy. In a 2002 article in *Christianity Today* entitled "Want Better Grades? Go to Church," Amber Anderson Johnson reported on a study conducted at an African-American Baptist church in New Orleans that continued to meet outdoors on folding chairs after the storm tore down the church building.

Children who continued to regularly attend the church received the following benefits:

- Access to material resources
- Access to supportive relationships
- Development of a desirable personal identity
- Experiences of power and control

- Experiences of social justice
- Adherence to cultural traditions
- Experiences of a sense of cohesion with others (Johnson 2002)

Creating Resilience through Recovery

Key to being a resilient person is realizing that many resilient characteristics are under our control, especially once we reach adulthood; we can consciously and proactively develop them. And the more we develop qualities of strength and resilience, the more insulated we are against the effects of trauma. It is entirely possible to go through painful life experiences and process as we go. When we do that, we actually build strength from facing and managing our own reactions to tough situations. Proactively building resilience includes processing what is in the way of it. (Crawford, Wright, and Masten 2005; Ungar et al 2007).

Optimism: A Resilience Enhancing Quality

In his presidential address to the American Psychological Association, psychologist Martin Seligman, one of the world's leading scholars on learned helplessness and depression, urged psychology to "turn toward understanding and building the human strengths to complement our emphasis on healing damage" (Seligman 1998, 1999). That speech launched today's positive psychology movement. Seligman also became one of the world's leading scholars on optimism. Optimists, says Seligman, see life through a positive lens. They see bad events as temporary setbacks or isolated to particular circumstances that can be overcome by their effort and abilities. Pessimists, on the other hand, react to setbacks from a presumption of personal helplessness. They feel that bad events are their fault, will last a long time, and will undermine everything they do (ibid).

Through his research, Seligman saw that the state of helplessness was a learned phenomenon. He also realized that un-helplessness could be learned as well. We could, in other words, learn to be optimists. He suggests that we learn to "hear" (and even write down) our beliefs about the events that block us from feeling good about ourselves or our lives and pay attention to the "recordings" we play in our head about them. Seligman also suggests we then write out the consequences of those beliefs—the toll they take on our emotions, energy, will to act, and the like. He suggests that once we become familiar with the pessimistic thought patterns we run through our heads, we challenge them (ibid). For example, we can challenge the usefulness of a specific belief and generate alternative ideas and solutions that might be better. We can choose to see problems as temporary, the way an optimist would, and that in itself provides psychological boundaries. This new type of thinking can stop the "loop" of negative tapes we run through our heads. Over time, this more optimistic thinking becomes engrained as our default position, and as we choose optimism over pessimism through repeated experiences, we are rewarded with new energy and vitality.

On the surface, this approach may appear to go directly against what we need to do in trauma resolution—that is, revisit and reexperience the traumatic moment or relational dynamic. But actually, the goal of healing is to create a shift in the way we see something and to reorganize our perception of previous events by incorporating our new learning into it. With this shift in perception, we open ourselves to new interpretations and reframing of past events.

Psychodrama, the type of role playing therapy that I specialize in, is a therapeutic intervention that can change the way we see things through working through personal stories. We play them out, reexamine the meaning that they had for us when we were helpless and create new meaning by looking at yesterday's circumstance through our more open and mature eyes of today. We recognize that we have a choice as to how to see the situation within the context of our lives.

Experiential therapy and 12-step programs help us to heal from emotional and psychological wounds, but this is not the whole story of healing. We also need to adopt the lifestyle changes that will make our gains sustainable and renewable.

FOURTEEN

Natural Highs: Bringing the Limbic System into Balance

When I stand before thee at the day's end, thou shalt see my scars and know that I had my wounds and also my healing.

—Rabindranath Tagore

O ur thoughts, emotions, and behaviors *all* affect our body chemistry. And our body chemistry affects our emotions and behavior. Just climbing out of bed in the morning and getting into a hot shower or bath, for example, elevates our levels of serotonin—"nature's natural antidepressant"—and makes it easier for us to get into a positive frame of mind. Here's what our bodies' natural antidepressants can do to help us to reduce stress and enhance health.

Serotonin keeps our moods balanced and upbeat. It calms anxiety and improves our sleep. Hot baths or showers give us a shot of *prolactin* (and serotonin), which is associated with that serene state that nursing mothers enter. Touching releases *oxytocin*, a bonding chemical that mediates emotional closeness and nourishes our brain. Paradoxically, oxytocin both helps us to feel close and connected *and* set boundaries. These are some of nature's mood stabilizers; they act in the brain and body in the same way that antidepressants act. They calm, soothe, and help us manage our moods.

When we don't make use of the medicine chest nature put inside of us and learn how to calm and soothe ourselves through daily, health-enhancing activities, we may want to turn to synthetic or artificial solutions to achieve a state of well-being. We might grab sugary or starchy foods or engage in compulsive sexual activities to get that dopamine release or use substances like alcohol or drugs to unwind, calm down, or de-stress.

Natural mood management amounts to paying attention to all of those little things that make us feel good because they are releasing soothing body chemicals into our bloodstreams and systematically building them into our daily routine. Walk to work, exercise with a friend, take time to relax, and just be. Breathe. We all know intuitively that certain activities just make us feel better, that creating an environment in which we feel relaxed and cozy calms and soothes us, and that taking time to unwind and pamper ourselves improves our attitude and the way we feel about ourselves. When we intentionally make these sorts of activities part of our daily lives, we're managing our moods the natural way and taking care of our mental and physical health. Rather than depending on synthetic mood managers that may be unhealthy or even self-destructive, we can depend on those that are natural, sustainable, and renewable to achieve and maintain emotional balance. So if you feel that you are doing all the right things and trying hard to understand your trauma issues but something just isn't kicking in for you, consider making the kind of lifestyle changes that are body/mind building blocks to a healthier, happier you.

Recovery, whether from a substance addiction, process addiction, or the trauma of being an ACoA, is about engaging in the kind of lifestyle behaviors that regulate brain and body chemistry. If you believe the ads on television, we should reach for a medication if we've been "sad, anxious, or depressed for two weeks or more."

Recovery is more than recovering from past pain. It is preventative mental health care. It is action-oriented and exists in the present. It is consciously building qualities of strength and resilience. Learning the skills of emotional literacy and balance allows us to work toward optimal mental and emotional strength and fitness, to be proactive about our mental health maintenance. This lifestyle is our best preventative against getting lost in the kinds of self-destructive and self-medicating behaviors that can undermine our happiness and our personal and professional success.

Processing old pain is only part of the puzzle of emotional wellness. Clients often feel that they are "working so hard" and have an improved understanding of their trauma-related issues—but they still feel stuck. This can be because their form of treatment isn't allowing them to really get to their core issues and process them or because they are sabotaging their recovery by making poor lifestyle choices. In other words, they are doing the necessary therapy to understand their trauma-related issues, but they are ignoring the needs of their bodies and not balancing their daily stressors with support and stress relief. It is worthwhile to take a look at what we do each day that may either be helping or hurting our cause. We can take a daily inventory of how much exercise we get, how much sleep we get, our network of relationships, the meaning and sense of purpose that drives us, and the amount of stress we have. This inventory allows us to see if our lifestyles are supporting or undermining our ability to actualize positive change. Then we figure out how to adopt healthy daily routines to allow our new changes to gain traction. If we have a good life container, our inner changes will have fertile soil in which to take root and grow.

Using the Body's Medicine Chest to Maintain Emotional Balance

Because human beings are always in a process of hurting and healing, nature has equipped us with a sort of self-care chemistry lab that's built into our brain and body. Learning to use that lab is the key to maintaining both emotional and physical health. It is entirely possible to attain that "feel good" state in a natural and healthy way if we just adopt a few proactive habits and consciously discipline ourselves to stay with them. Regular exercise can be a powerful antidepressant and is linked with decreased anxiety, stress, and hostility (Otto and Smits 2011). Calming body chemicals like serotonin and dopamine are nature's natural mood stabilizers; they calm us down, smooth out our rough edges, and help us to feel good. We can learn to use these *chemicals of emotion* to our advantage. Our brains produce more than fifty known active drugs that influence our memory and intelligence and act as natural sedatives. In other words, we can learn to adopt activities that stimulate these natural drugs in a way that enhance our health rather than undermine it. We can learn to self-medicate the healthy way!

Brain Overload: Feeling Stressed and Self-Sabotaging Food Choices

In the same way that our physical muscles get tired after a tough workout and require rest to recuperate, our mental muscles need rest and relaxation so that they can function optimally. Just as a bicep muscle has practical limitations, so does the muscle of the brain. If we ask our muscles to hold more weight than they are able to support, they will eventually give out.

An interesting Stanford University study involving "brain overload" and described in a *Wall Street Journal* article may shed light on why we need regular breaks to stay resilient and make healthy choices. Several dozen undergraduates were divided into two groups; one group was given a five-digit number to remember while the second group was given a seven-digit number. They were then told to walk down the hall where they were given two different snack options: a slice of chocolate cake or a bowl of fruit salad. The students with seven digits to remember were nearly twice as likely to choose the cake, while the students given only five digits to remember (a more manageable load) were still relaxed enough to reach for the fruit they knew was better for them. Mental stress and the anxiety created by that bit of extra stuff to remember led straight to poor food choices. The reason, according to Professor Baba Shiv, who conducted the experiment, was that the extra numbers took up valuable space in the brain and became a "cognitive load" (Lehrer 2009). When we're already feeling overwhelmed, we seem to continue on that path; the prefrontal cortex gets so overtaxed that all it takes is a few extra bits of information before the brain starts to give in to temptation.

In a 2002 experiment, led by Mark Muraven at the University at Albany, a group of male subjects was asked to not think about a white elephant for five minutes while writing down their thoughts. That turns out to be a rather difficult mental challenge, akin to staying focused on a tedious project at work. (A control group was given a few simple arithmetic problems to solve.) Then, Mr. Muraven had the subjects take a beer taste test, although he warned them that their next task involved driving a car. Sure enough, people in the white elephant group drank significantly more beer than people in the control group, which suggests that they had a harder time not indulging in alcohol (ibid).

"A tired brain preoccupied with its problems is going to struggle to resist what it wants, even when what it wants isn't what we need" (ibid). This kind of mental stress overload can affect all sorts of little choices that we make throughout our day that are related to self-medicating behaviors.

Members of an alcoholic/addicted family carry a great deal of psychological and emotional weight that stresses our mental muscles. Denying is also stressful; as we try to figure out whether or not to deal with that "pink elephant in the living room," our muscles for living "normally" lose their resilience and strength. This is why self-care and surrender are so important in recovery. We need to surrender to the recognition that we cannot carry more than we can carry and build back our resilience and strength in our mental and emotional muscles so that we can begin to make healthy, healing choices for ourselves.

What Is Self-Care, Anyway?

Our emotions and our bodies are so closely linked that taking care of the body is taking care of the mind, and taking care of the mind is taking care of the body. Both are crucial to emotional health.

Trauma can undermine our motivation to take care of ourselves, particularly in the areas of hygiene, rest, good nutrition, and exercise. After a traumatic experience, people often lose some maturational achievements and regress to earlier modes of coping with stress. In children, this may show up as an inability to take care of themselves in such areas as feeding and toilet training; in adults, it is expressed in excessive dependence and in a loss of capacity to make thoughtful, autonomous decisions. (van der Kolk 1994). The recovery process can also put us under extra strain and at times be somewhat regressive. As we revisit childhood pain and vulnerability, we revisit our childhood states. For this reason, extra attention to self-care is an important part of getting back on track and staying on track. Adopting lifestyle changes that not only heal the body mind but also are strategies for sustaining mental and emotional health while processing painful situations as they occur—our ultimate goal in recovery.

Why wait to get sick before we get help? We have learned that lowering our cholesterol reduces heart disease. There is such a thing as emotional cholesterol, too. Following are a variety of ways to keep our emotional cholesterol low so we can stay mentally and emotionally fit.

Your Well-Being Checklist: Are You Getting Enough . . . ?

- **Good Food.** Eat well: eat a balanced diet and stay away from excess sugar, white flour, and caffeine. Stress depletes dopamine and so does lack of sleep and poor nutrition. Alcohol, caffeine, and sugar all appear to decrease dopamine levels in the brain. Some foods, however, actually increase dopamine levels and get that magical medicine chest working in our favor. Foods like avocados, almonds, bananas, dairy products, pumpkin and sesame seeds, and legumes are the ones to reach for.

- **Exercise.** Research studies found that exercising, such as brisk walking three to four times a week, can have the same mood-elevating results as medication when it comes to treating depression.

- **Sleep and Rest.** Get enough sleep: we need sufficient sleep to give our nervous systems, muscles, and minds the rest they require to function well. Lack of proper sleep can exacerbate depression and anxiety and lead to low energy levels, mood swings, and a lack of ability to concentrate.

- **Oxygen.** Breathe: scientists have discovered that oxygen is critical for the production of adenosine triphosphate (ATP), a high-energy molecule that stores the energy our bodies need to do just about everything. ATP releases energy when it is broken down (hydrolyzed) into ADP (or adenosine diphosphate). Because this energy is used for many metabolic processes it is considered the universal energy currency for metabolism. Oxygen is the most vital component in ATP production. And if something goes wrong with the production of ATP, the result is lowered vitality, disease, and premature aging.[citation t/k from author]

- **Yoga/Meditation.** Yoga exercises increase respiratory efficiency, normalize gastrointestinal functions, and increase muscle and skeletal flexibility and joint range of motion, and meditation trains us to calm the mind and body.

- **Sunlight.** Get thirty minutes of sunlight a day. Sunlight, because it contains vitamin D, helps prevent cancer, bone disease, depression, and many other illnesses that are only now beginning to be understood. Also, because vitamin D can help lower and control insulin, sunlight may also play a role in helping us reach our weight-loss goals.

- **Connection:** As Margaret Mead said, "Having someone wonder where you are when you don't come home at night is a very old human need." Humans are pack animals, and we apparently experience health benefits, including longer lives, if we have a network of supportive relationships. In a study done in Canada, a sense of community proved to have beneficial effects on people's health. It was concluded that a sense of belonging might be part of health prevention (MacPherson et al 2006). This is currently an area of study and research and results may vary from study to study, gender to gender, and culture to culture, but across the board, relationships clearly play a role in longevity.

- **Positivity.** Maintain a positive attitude: researchers at the University of Texas found that people with an upbeat view of life were less likely than pessimists to show signs of frailty. They speculate that positive emotions may directly affect health by altering the chemical balance of the body. Alternatively, it may be that an upbeat attitude helps to boost a person's health by making it more likely they will feel good about themselves and their lives. (Leath 1999).

- **Self-Soothing.** Take a bath: a warm bath releases prolactin, the same soothing hormone released by nursing mothers. Massage releases oxytocin—nature's "brain fertilizer" that actually causes neurons to connect and grow.

- **Unloading.** Journal, pray, or share your feelings: all of these activities enhance immune function (Pennebaker 1997, Dossey1993).

- **Meaningful Activity.** Rather that straining to "find a passion," try being passionate about what you find. Our capacity for depth and engagement can be applied to and repeated with a number of meaningful activities throughout our life spans. Have some goals that allow you to feel purposeful; develop a self-reflectiveness that can give life a sense of meaning and beauty. A sense of appreciation and gratitude are consistently correlated with happiness and health.

- **Therapeutic Support Systems:** The kind of trauma that occurs in childhood and evidences itself through the symptoms that we discussed in our chapters on relationship trauma does not tend to get better on its own. Its roots are deep, and once we begin dealing with it, we need a reliable support network. The kind of deep sharing that goes on in group therapy actually elevates the immune system and acts as a destressor.

Breathe, Breathe, Breathe

If you feel yourself beginning to enter that emotionally frayed and fried zone, try some simple mood-managing strategies. Next time you're sitting in front of your computer and your body morphs into a vibrating mass of nervous little pricks or you hear one more piece of lousy financial news and your gut starts to glue itself to the inside wall of your stomach, simply breathe in slowly and mindfully and bring your mind into the here and now in the present. Slow down your breathing, relax your muscles, and calm your nervous system.

The breath connects the body and the mind, so slowing down the breath has the effect of calming the body, mind, and emotions. Breathing is a bodily function that is regulated by the autonomic nervous system as well as the conscious voluntary nervous system. Breathing is the only body function that creates a bridge between the conscious and unconscious mind/

body, bringing them into a mutual balance.

Sometimes our fear and hypervigilance makes us hold our breath. When our brains anticipate danger or we get scared, our breathing rate increases so that more oxygen can be sent to the blood cells and muscle fibers to prepare us to fight or run away to safety. In either case we can try to relax ourselves consciously by slowing down and deepening our inhalations and exhalations, thereby stimulating our relaxation response and calming our emotions.

Try it for yourself right now. Simply draw deep, rhythmic breaths, allow your diaphragm to expand as you do this, and observe calm coming into your body, mind, and emotions. Then loosen up your mind. As your breath helps you to even out your mood, allow your mind to move toward or away from what is preoccupying it without getting caught up in or stuck in it. Other techniques are to allow your thoughts to simply pass by the inner eye of your mind as if you were sitting on the banks of a river watching the water carry them downstream, or release them as if they were floating up into the clouds and being carried away by a gentle breeze.

Why Exercise Is a Natural Antidepressant

Endorphins are the body's sedatives and also act as painkillers, diminishing our perception of pain. When we are hurt and endorphins are released, they have an analgesic effect that is far more potent than morphine. This effect allows us to feel empowered and to function. Endorphins are manufactured in our brain, spinal cord, and many other parts of our bodies. Not coincidently, the neuron receptors that endorphins bind to are the same ones that bind to some pain medicines. However, unlike morphine, the activation of these receptors by the body's own endorphins does not lead to addiction, dependence, or negative lifestyle patterns.

Exercise boosts the brain's feel-good endorphins, releases muscle tension, improves sleep, and reduces levels of the stress hormone cortisol. It also increases our body temperature, which may have a calming effect. All of these changes in our mind and body can improve such symptoms as sadness, anxiety, irritability, stress, fatigue, anger, self-doubt, helplessness, and hopelessness—all of which are associated with depression (Singh et al).

Though research suggests that it may take at least thirty minutes of exercise a day, three to five times a week, to significantly improve depression symptoms, any amount of activity—as little as ten to fifteen minutes at a time—can still improve mood in the short term. Research also shows that we're more likely to maintain good exercise habits if we get exercise to fit into our lives—for example, by walking or biking to work, or by walking, jogging, or playing a sport with friends (Blumenthal et al 1999).

Exercise is proactive. Along with the obvious physiological benefits, it is helpful psychologically to feel that we can do something each day to help ourselves. So walk, bike, play a sport, go to a yoga class, or dance around your house to your favorite music. It's fun, relaxing, and good for your body, mind, and soul.

Studies on Exercise, Anxiety, and Depression

The science behind just how and why exercise can help to reduce symptoms of anxiety and depression has been a much-studied topic over the last two decades.

In a Duke University research study published in the October 25, 1999, issue of the *Archives of Internal Medicine,* exercise was found to be almost as effective as medication in reducing symptoms of depression. In the study, 156 patients diagnosed with major depressive disorder were divided into three groups to study the impact that exercise might have on depression: Group one exercised. Group two used medication. Group three used a combination of medication and exercise. Much to the surprise of the researchers, after sixteen weeks all three groups showed similar and significant improvements in their depression. Here are the statistical findings of the study:

- 60.4 percent of the group who did exercise alone were no longer depressed after sixteen weeks.
- 65.5 percent of the group who used medication alone were no longer depressed after sixteen weeks.
- 68.8 percent of the group who did both exercise and medication were no longer depressed after sixteen weeks.

The researchers did note that patients who took the antidepressants (in this case Zoloft) saw their symptoms relieved sooner, but by sixteen weeks the group differences had virtually disappeared.

Though medication can be a lifesaver for some, and no one wants to suggest otherwise, these studies open the door for alternative or additional strategies. "One of the conclusions we can draw from this," according to psychologist and study leader Dr. James Blumenthal, "is that exercise may be just as effective as medication and may be a better alternative for certain patients. While we don't know why exercise confers such a benefit, this study shows that exercise should be considered as a credible form of treatment for these patients. Almost one-third of depressed patients in general do not respond to medications, and for others, the medications can cause unwanted side effects. Exercise should be considered a viable option."

Depression also has a social side. People who are depressed or socially anxious tend to isolate. "So it's possible," reflected Blumenthal, "that the structured and supportive atmosphere of the exercise program could have contributed to improving the symptoms of the exercise group."

Blumenthal also feels that exercise may be beneficial because patients are actually taking a proactive role in their own physical and psychological health. "Taking a pill is . . . passive," he says. "Patients who exercised may have felt a greater sense of mastery over their condition and gained a greater sense of accomplishment. They may have felt more self-confident and had better self-esteem because they were able to do it themselves, and they may have attributed their improvement to their ability to exercise. These findings could change the way some depressed patients are treated, especially those who are not interested in taking antidepressants," Blumenthal goes on to say. "Although these medications have been proven to be effective, many people want to avoid the side effects or are looking for a more 'natural' way to feel better."

However, there is such a thing as overexercising or too much of a good thing. Because exercise is a natural high, people can go overboard with it.

Compulsive exercising can mean that one is using exercise to the extreme, which starts to diminish its emotional benefits. Walking several times a week keeps us active and stimulates the kinds of hormones that elevate and soothe moods naturally. But compulsive exercise starts to have diminishing returns. Some signs that we're exercising too much are exercising at length; when we're feeling unwell; at a vigorous intensity; or in unusual places, such as in bed or in the middle of the night, as a pattern of hiding begins. When we feel guilty or anxious if we miss an exercise session, double our exercise to make up for it, or miss socializing because of too much time at the gym, we may be overdoing it. Too much exercise can injure bones and stress the body. Overexercise can become a process addiction as with any behavior that is done to excess. As with anything in life, the secret is in finding the right balance (Blumenthal et al 1999).

Put Meaning and Purpose into Your Life

The feeling that we are making a positive contribution to our world that connects us to others who are making similar contributions is an esteem-building activity that makes us feel good about ourselves. "Well-being is a process (of staying well), not an end-state, so any conceptualization of well-being that concentrates on end-states . . . is probably off track. It may be that in some cultures well-being is characterized by self-acceptance, positive relations with others, autonomy, environmental mastery, purpose in life, and personal growth" (Leath 1999). We build resilience throughout life when we can mobilize our circumstances to meet our needs and engage with others in meeting theirs; it is the circle of life.

"Purpose in life involves having clear perceptions of what kind of far-off yet potentially achievable future experience will bring about rewarding experience. Meaning in life, however, does not necessarily involve sustained focus on particular goals" (ibid).

Developing a sense of meaning is not only intellectual; it involves engaging in activities that create meaning, and it is different for different people and different cultures. We are all naturally engaged in a process by which we assign meaning to our lives based on what we have experienced in the past, what we have learned through experience, what plans for the future we can formulate, and our willingness and ability to work toward actualizing those plans.

Maintain the Right Ratio
of Positive versus Negative Emotions

Barbara Fredrickson, a social psychologist at the University of North Carolina at Chapel Hill and author of *Positivity*, writes about what makes for an upbeat outlook on life. In her research, Fredrickson found that it is important to actively maintain a conscious balance between our negative and positive emotions in order to sustain a positive attitude. "Our emotions tend to obey a tipping point," she writes. That tipping point among Americans tends to be a 3-to-1. "We need three positive emotions to lift us up for every one negative emotion that brings us down" (Fredrickson 2009). To improve the ratio, Fredrickson feels that we need to give ourselves time to do the things that we enjoy and to live more in the present. "Resilient people manage adversity and handle unexpected things. It's not just that they only experience positive emotions, but instead that they are able to cultivate more positive feelings. Resilient people don't make social comparisons. Instead they focus on what's positive in their own lives" (ibid).

Twelve-step programs talk about "comparing and despairing" or "comparing our insides to other people's outsides." Keeping the focus on ourselves and being grateful for what we have rather than bemoaning what others have that we lack ups our positivity ratio, which ups our mood and frame of mind. Fredrickson's research shows that "Positivity reigns whenever positive emotions—like love, joy, gratitude, serenity, interest, and inspiration—touch and open your heart. One of the most positive emotions to elicit is gratitude. . . . If we see what we are going through as a gift or an opportunity it unlocks that positive emotion" (ibid).

So keep a journal and a gratitude list, say a prayer, or walk outdoors with a friend and share what's on your mind. Get the help you need when you need it, and engage in the kinds of activities that give you a sense of pleasure and meaning. Research bears out that these activities work on the brain in a similar way as brain meds, and they can even have better, lasting results because, when you're personally proactive, you're actively taking charge of your own emotional health.

PART V:

Integrating the Fragmented Self

Life is difficult. This is a great truth, one of the greatest truths. It is a great truth because once we truly see this truth, we transcend it. Once we truly know that life is difficult—once we truly understand and accept it—then life is no longer difficult. Because once it is accepted, the fact that life is difficult no longer matters.

—M. Scott Peck

FIFTEEN

Relationships:
Recover or Repeat

*It is my absolute belief that authentic change begins
with self-responsibility and the courage to peruse
what is right and effective even when the people
beyond us may not cooperate or support our efforts.
Being willing to face our own limitations and work
diligently to become the best people we can be,
despite our legitimate sorrows, is the only path
to genuine fulfillment that I know, and a
prerequisite to creating successful relationships.*

—Nina Brown, *Children of the Self-Absorbed*

O ur emotions are put under the microscope when we enter
a deep, committed relationship. The magnetic pull of intimate bonding draws parts of us toward the surface of our being
that may be far from our everyday consciousness. In intimate part-
nership we are thrown back upon our childhood selves, reliving
the pleasure, comfort, and excitement we had when life was new
and fresh. We find ourselves feeling and sometimes acting like

children—vulnerable, dependent, and daring to dream. When we join hands with another person, we create an intimate space where young parts of us come forward; where we can regress into a playful and innocent state of mind; where we can giggle, cuddle, and coo and have a cozy little world that belongs only to two. A special and protective space where we can not only be more than our ordinary selves—generous, forgiving, and high-minded—but less as well, where we can be vulnerable and shaky, stumbling over our faults and fears and have a hand outstretched as we ask for help in hoisting ourselves back up again.

Because our renewed bonds of intimacy draw forward our deepest yearnings to be seen, understood, loved, and valued, they also touch on the unfulfilled longings and old hurts also associated with those early bonds. For the ACoA, this is where the rubber meets the road. Those very feelings of vulnerability and dependence that allow us to reenter a barely remembered world in which we feel safe and held can also reignite unresolved relationship wounds.

The limbic bonds with parents and siblings that held our relationships in place throughout childhood get formed once again with our partners and children through the proximity of physical and emotional closeness. And those bonds carry with them the memory of what it meant to be close, sometimes in surprising detail. What we experienced as children; what we thought was ancient history—both in the realms of pleasure and pain—pulls at forgotten corners of our minds and hearts, bringing with it both fantasies and fears of what we might experience as we get close. We may dream that a relationship will make us feel whole, end our yearnings for belonging, solve our lives, and help us to fulfill that age-old goal of living happily after. But at the same time we can fear being swallowed up and digested into someone else's being, feeling trapped inside someone else's life, unable to find ourselves and who we once were. While these fears are natural in anyone, childhood trauma can make them feel over-whelming at times.

When Our Inner Child Falls in Love

It is part of a healthy and happy intimacy that the "child" mind and heart are alive and well. After all, it is the child in us who trusts and loves and plays, who can feel thrilled with the little things of life that make up a pleasant day. This is a gift of inti-mate love. But it can also be the Trojan horse that lets loose all sorts of warring parts of us.

We carry the conflated but unconscious imagery from our past in our child trauma mind. Ever vibrating beneath the thin mem-brane of experience is the drunk mother threatening to burst out, the drunk dad throwing a tantrum, or the chaos or discon-nection of the family of origin threatening to surface. Even when ACoAs or their partners do not drink or drug, the unconscious memory of those that did can be a ghostlike presence that never gets talked about. Because what would you say? And how would you say it? You might feel like you are babbling incoherently, just stirring up trouble and that old "walking on egg shells" feel-ing might come back and make the whole subject feel a little dangerous and out of bounds.

The past and present images become conflated and indistinguishable from each other, and we are at risk for making our relationship hold not only the weight of today's conflict, but the weight of our unresolved history.

We feel overwhelmed by the same feelings of helplessness, rage, and choicelessness that we experienced as a child, and we completely lose track of the fact that we are now adults and can think with the mind of a mature and thoughtful person. That child we once were gets warmed up, and we cry her little tears along with ours; we fight his battles holding up a plastic shield; we feel small and defenseless all over again in the presence of this big love. Or we want to run out of the house feeling hurt and misunderstood and hide under a tree or in a corner. Or we feel outraged and cannot integrate, manage, or own the feeling that is so threatening to the child mind to acknowledge.

So far, we might be describing what happens in any fight between members of a couple. We all have little kids inside of us—we're supposed to. But when we add the triggered contents of a "dissociated self" to the fight, we now have a potent blast of unconscious emotion, interpretation, and possible behaviors to contend with. Like a tiger suddenly wakened out of a deep sleep, we can become enraged and out of control if we are touched in a way that pushes on an unhealed wound and makes it hurt all over again. We rise up, sword in hand, to fight the unfought battles of our youth, not even noticing where our blade lands and draws blood. In those moments of triggered, blind rage, all we see is a target for our pain and resentment.

If both people have these sore spots (which is the case more often than not), then a regular fight can go from zero to ten in a heartbeat. Because what is out of sight is not necessarily out of mind, and what we don't know can still hurt us.

We can operate in our relationships, informed by our childhood conceptions and misconceptions of events, well into adulthood. We become glued to our past interpretations of events, defending them as if our lives depended upon it, feeling as if letting go of our point of view is letting go of some piece of ourselves that we will never get back. Our defenses, like the pain that got triggered, become immature and impenetrable. We are stuck in our own story.

Transference: Entering Emotional Quicksand

When we are triggered by something that "reminds" us of a time in our lives when we might have felt helpless, scared, and vulnerable, we become lost in a web of disequilibrating emotions, not knowing how to sort them out or come back from them. We can become pugnacious and ready for battle or silent and withdrawn; we explode or implode. The danger is that ACoAs may feel that the intensity of their emotional response is entirely driven by what is happening in the present moment that triggered them. They may remain unconscious and unaware that yesterday's wounds are bleeding into today. In an article titled "Control, Attachment Style, and Relationship Satisfaction Among Adult Children of Alcoholics," published in the *Journal of Mental Health Counseling*, authors Denise Beesley and Cal D.

Stoltenberg discuss "how ACoAs develop coping habits that may include an exaggerated need to control situations and/or people in order to 'mediate the chaos and unpredictability' of the alcoholic families in which they grow up that they then 'transport' into adult relationships" (2002). Although in the short term these seem adaptive maneuvers, in the long run, when carried into adult relationships, they become maladaptive (Ackerman 1987). Research suggests that "'ACoAs' inability to express their needs and feelings are based on ingrained patterns of distrust, secretiveness, and fear of intimacy and abandonment and that the interpersonal difficulties of ACoAs are reflective of the relational patterns in the alcoholic family of origin. Over time these patterns become the foundation for negative expectations about establishing and maintaining secure relationships" (El-Guebaly et al 1993).

When Geneva and Rashid have a fight, they can quickly become enraged. In the blink of an eye, Geneva becomes Rashid's alcoholic mother and Rashid becomes Geneva's raging father. Geneva feels threatened by Rashid's anger way before it turns into rage. Small signs that his anger is escalating, like leaning forward in his chair, waving his arms, redness in his face, or his voice getting tense and louder, send Geneva straight into defensive behaviors. She becomes suddenly critical and insulting of Rashid; underneath she is quaking, but on the surface she is aggressive. Meanwhile, the more critical Geneva gets the more she triggers Rashid's unconscious memories of his mother's drunken states when she was critical and nasty. This web of unconscious recollections quickly wraps itself in and around Rashid's thinking, and he projects the full package onto Geneva. No longer is she the critical spouse reacting to his accelerating anger . . . she becomes, in Rashid's mind, a drunk mother humiliating him. In the unconsciousness of the moment, the power balance shifts completely as Rashid seamlessly slips into his child self and reacts to the present as if it were his past. He actually feels like a little boy dealing with a huge, drunken mother. But he doesn't know that. And the further he becomes stuck to this web of unconscious recollections, the more Geneva "sees" him as the reincarnation of her raging father acting through the body of her husband and the more stubborn she becomes. But she doesn't know it either.

They don't know because they have not made their unconscious wounds conscious, so they are left to mindlessly project their unresolved pain onto their adult relationships—thus recreating and reliving the past in the present over and over again. And the more they have this same fight, the more the past actually does become the present. Yesterday's pain is re-created and lived out today and passed along into tomorrow.

In other words, when we're triggered we become overcome by the past and unable to function or gather new information in the present, because "emergence of the dissociative capsule into the present moment would destroy its function (intentionality, acquisition of new memory and evolution of the sense of self)" (Scaer 2007). The present moment becomes, in a sense, dysfunctional, consumed by past, unresolved trauma-based recollections that consist of "old emotionally based declarative memories and feelings from the body reflecting the autonomic, emotional and somatic input from traumatic procedural memory" (ibid). Rashid and Geneva were no longer arguing with each other; they were arguing with ghosts from their past. "During this obliteration of the present moment, the person would exist in the past traumatic experience, would respond to its messages as if confronted with the old trauma, and would be unable to form plans of action or store new memories based on current experience" (ibid).

When these disowned parts of ourselves get triggered by some sort of situation or dynamic that pulls them forward or restimulates them, we may still have trouble owning and coming to terms with them. The moment feeling them starts to hurt, we swing into action, ready for fight or flight—but we don't really know why. We go into our heads, blame others or project so that we can avoid feeling the layers of pain underneath what is being triggered. And we see the culprit as whatever or whomever is triggering us, which, over time, has the effect of distancing us even further from our own inner truths and drivers. We become not only more distant from our partners, but more distant from ourselves. In terms of intimacy, we are making two significant mistakes: first, we're not owning what's in us and taking responsibility for whatever unresolved pain from the past we are importing into our relationship and growing from this knowledge of what lies within our unconscious; and second, we're transferring our past onto our present and mixing our partner up with our parent. Even though our partner may naturally share similar qualities, he or she simply is not that parent.

When couples fight and trigger each other, they may both get caught in this loop. They may both be "living in the past" psychologically and emotionally. They may be getting locked into a transference reaction from the past and completely unable to take in the kind of new information that might allow them to listen to their partner and solve the problem. They lose their ability to be present-oriented and talk about what is really going on for them. They are shadowboxing with someone from the past.

Bringing Our Inner Adult Back Online

Couples need to understand each other's triggers. They also need to accept that their traumatized child mind is a place from which they will see each other. They may experience themselves as small and their partner as large or they may sink into a collapsed and helpless place seeing their partner as having all the power, and they may have trouble owning how scared, hurt, and angry they are. When two people are triggered at the same time, the animal mind (the limbic, feeling/sensing mind) is in charge, and the thinking mind goes off-line. We're in our "trauma trap." We become trapped in our own trauma transference and our interaction is, at least momentarily, held hostage to past relationships. Understanding the forces that form the relational template and the transferences and projections that we carry and constantly re-create, is one of the most liberating things we can do for ourselves or for our relationship. At those moments, we need to remember to not make our partner in the present responsible for all of our feelings from the past.

When couples get into this place, they need to take a break to breathe, breathe, breathe. Taking a moment to separate and breathe is a simple but very effective strategy that allows the nervous system to restore balance and the limbic storm to pass. The triggered ACoAs can then return to the present where they can again think and make choices that might allow them to move through a trigger moment. Their thinking minds can come back onboard as their limbic worlds quiet down. They can then grow from these triggered moments rather than simply get lost in reliving them over and over again.

How to Turn Triggered Moments into Growth Moments

The Fight: Solution A. We get triggered by the intense feelings accompanying intimacy, so we:

- Blame our partner (or children) for what we are feeling.
- Make our pain about our partner (or child) rather than recognizing that the intensity of our reaction may have historical fuel.
- Feel like a victim, see our partner (or even our children) as the aggressor and ourselves as the disempowered victim.
- Collapse into helplessness and/or become aggressive and intimidate our partner or children.

We become disappointed, see the other person as wrong, or withdraw or rage—or a combination of these. Rage versus cold withdrawal are really two sides of the same coin. Each serves the function of allowing us to maintain our distance. Both rage and cold withdrawal are hurtful to our partner. We grow more distant from our partner and the gulf between us grows.

The Fight: Solution B. We get triggered by the intense feelings accompanying intimacy, so we:

- Blame our partner (or children) for what we are feeling.
- Make our pain about our partner (or child) rather than recognizing that the intensity of our reaction may have historical fuel.
- Feel like a victim; see our partner (or even our children) as the aggressor and ourselves as the disempowered victim.
- Collapse into helplessness and/or become aggressive and intimidate our partner or children.

But then, we back up and, breathe, breathe, breathe. We settle down and pull our focus off of the other person and back toward ourselves. We check in with what's really going on with us. We take responsibility for what we're feeling and use it to better understand who we are so that we can grow personally. We try to explain ourselves to our partner, tell him or her what triggered us, and separate the past from the present through understanding how much of our reaction is historical and how much is about real issues of today that need to be addressed. We listen to our partner do the same. We talk things over with a more calm and rational mind/body. We grow as a person and as a couple and feel closer having come into a relational balance together.

Turning the Tide

Admitting to our own transferences, seeing them for what they are, and seeing how they shape and set up our expectations of others are important parts of trauma resolution. When we project what we fear the most onto those close to us again and again, we may unwittingly participate in creating it. Even though another person may well be reminding us of some part of an early, primary relationship dynamic, that person is not the earlier person. But our trauma transference mind doesn't know this; it relentlessly paints in the rest of the picture in excruciating detail and reacts to that picture as if it were the whole story, and soon all we see, all we expect, and all we allow, is what we got. We cannot move beyond the internal map we have drawn; we're stuck in our own picture from the past. Like placing the negative from an old photo on top of a new one, the past and the present blur into each other and we are not capable of being in the here and now. We are in our dissociated capsule, seeing only what we saw, feeling only what we felt, and doing only what we did or wished we could do. We scream and rail at a ghost.

SIXTEEN

Grandchildren of Addiction: Breaking the Chain

What was silent in the father speaks in the son, and I have often found in the son the unveiled secret of the father.

—Friedrich Nietzche

Is it addiction that "skips" a generation or does trauma become intergenerational? It has long been speculated that alcoholism "skips" a generation. But when we understand how ACoAs who become parents may import and live out the ACoA trauma syndrome in their parenting, we need to question what exactly is skipping a generation: an "alcoholic gene" or their unresolved CoA pain? Or both?

Our children become who we are, not who we tell them to be; if we want to change our children, we need to change ourselves. We need to take recovery from the ACoA trauma syndrome as seriously as recovery from mood-altering substances.

ACoAs do not need to be self-medicators to pass on pain. ACoAs may play out alcoholic family dynamics whether or not alcohol is present in spite of their best efforts to avoid doing that. As parents, they may overreact or underreact. The ACoA's style of parenting may reflect the same lack of regulation that is part of the ACoA trauma syndrome; it may seesaw, for example, between enmeshment and disengagement or chaos and rigidity. The same unregulated family dynamics that the ACoA learned while growing up get re-created in the ACoA's own parenting.

This is why being a *grandchild* of an alcoholic/addicted family can be as if not more confusing than being a *child* of an alcoholic/addicted family. Grandchildren experience the residue of their parent's untreated PTSD issues, but there is no obvious culprit causing it: after all, no one is drunk, right? But ACoAs can be emotionally drunk. If ACoAs do not treat their own PTSD issues, they are at high risk for re-creating many of the types of dynamics that they grew up with in their own partnering and parenting, in one form of another. They likely do this without awareness, truly convinced that they are delivering the kind of care and attention that they never got. The problem is that their caring and loyalty may be fueled by some of their own unconscious and unmet needs and their children sense this and feel guilty and even resentful—but they don't know why. If they felt underparented, for example, they may overparent; if they felt underprotected, they may overprotect; if they felt kept at a distance, they may even glue themselves to their children, suffocating them with more attention of a certain kind than is healthy. Thus, the grandchild of alcoholics (GCoA) inherits the dynamics that are trauma-related without the obvious trauma; because of this, they may feel guilty over their parents' tough past but confused about how their parents might be passing pain along to them. In this way, the torch of dysfunction gets transmitted to another generation and may set the GCoA up for wanting to self-medicate. Addiction, in other words, skips a generation (T. Dayton 2007).

Grandchildren of addiction pick up on the unhealed pain of their ACoA parents, and because of that they may carry silent worries. Aware of their parents' tough childhoods, they can feel guilty and not really know why. They can feel guilty about their natural mixture of positive and negative feelings toward their parents that are part of any close relationship, or disloyal because they want their own lives in which their parents are not a central focus. After all, they are lucky, right? Their poor parents had all this pain and would never treat their children like they were treated. Right? But their ACoA parents may well be passing along a more silent form of pain—the unhealed PTSD of their past. Children absorb their parent's love, joy, and pleasure in life through the natural phenomenon of limbic resonance. They also absorb sadness, guilt, and anger; whether it is spoken or not, they "carry their parent's pain."

And one of the problems is that ACoAs oftentimes do not think they need help. The defenses against feeling and processing pain that they developed early in childhood have become part of their personalities. Their pain is so well hidden, so well intellectualized, that they are caught in their own trap. The trap is that because ACoAs often have the capacity to understand what happened to them, they mistake intellectual understanding for emotional processing; their pain remains unprocessed; they can refer to it but do not feel it, and they block it in a thousand clever ways. ACoAs also may continue to live out their caretaking patterns from childhood in parenting, such as identifying in someone else what needs fixing in them.

Parents with a family history of trauma and/or addiction may tend to:

- Have trouble tolerating their children's intense feelings because they have trouble tolerating their own.

- Have trouble tolerating their children being rejected by anyone.

- Have problems with their own self-regulation that impact how they deal with their children's ups and downs.

- May violate their children's boundaries by being unnecessarily intrusive and overly curious about their children's affairs.

- Either read too much and overreact to situations that bother their children, or block their overreaction and underreact instead.

- Overprotect their children even when it is not in their children's best interest.

- Not know what normal is and consequently have trouble understanding which behaviors to accept or foster as normal in their children and which behaviors to discourage.

- Have trouble having relaxed and easy fun with their children.

- Have impulsive features that they act out in their parenting.

- Feel somewhat different from other families.

- Attempt to overcontrol family life and the lives of their children.

- Have trouble establishing healthy boundaries with their children, positioning themselves either too close or too far. (T. Dayton 2007).

ACoAs may look to their own children to fill the emotional void left by pain from their own past:

- GCoAs may carry a sense of guilt for their parents' painful past.
- GCoAs may feel "crazy" because, while there is nothing like addiction or abuse occurring in their families, their parents are passing on pain through their own unexamined PTSD-related issues.
- ACoAs may pass on their tendency toward traumatic bonding to their children; they may become overclose or cycle between over- and underclose because they themselves lack a sense of normal (T. Dayton 2007).

GCoAs may carry a sense that something is wrong with them that they can't quite put their finger on. If their parents have grudges, resentments, or disconnects with their own parents and siblings, GCoAs may have loyalty issues or inherit relationship "shadows" with their aunts, uncles, grandparents, or cousins. And there are other invisible issues that GCoAs absorb through their parents' silent pain. According to Ann W. Smith, author of *Grandchildren of Alcoholics: Another Generation of Codependency,*

> *GCoAs show similar signs of dysfunction and trauma as their ACoA parents, although they may never have seen or known about the addict in the family. While their ACoA parents put great effort into overcoming what they experienced as children, despite this effort, they silently transmit the dynamics and emotions of their childhood by example and through the unconscious patterns of attachment that they*

developed early in life. They cover their pain and create what appears to be a close, healthy family. The ACOA's efforts to improve family life for their children are aimed at doing the right things but none the less, as they grow up, the grandchildren often resurrect the very same issues that their ACOA parents were running away from. They exhibit low self-worth, external focus, difficulty managing emotions and problems with relationships. When the GCoA runs into trouble as an adult he or she assumes it is personal failure. They do not have a story that justifies their deficiencies and are very protective of their parents who tried so hard. They must shoulder their burden alone until they get help and discover the intergenerational basis of their difficulties.

- GCoAs may have some trouble "right sizing" their emotional reactions having grown up around their ACoA parent's emotional dysregulation.
- GCoAs may experience some fear around committed relationships as they are hyperaware of what can go wrong.
- GCoAs may have trouble setting their own boundaries as their ACoA parents may have cycled between over-closeness and under-closeness or because the closeness with their parents was based on the parent's need rather than their own.
- GCoAs may have trouble separating and individuating, as their ACoA parents may have also had issues in this area.
- GCoAs may feel somewhat different from their friends who did not carry their parents' pain.
- GCoAs may have so much anxiety around getting things right that it can resurface in relationships, work, or the social world.

On the positive side, GCoAs have often been raised by ACoA parents who are deeply devoted to them. Having been hurt as children, ACoA parents can be determined to do their best by their kids and can give them much love, understanding, and attention. ACoA parents may also be very generous and supportive of their children with both their time and their financial resources. As a result, GCoAs can feel highly valued by their parents. This feature alone becomes core to their sense of self and is a great buffer against other less desirable features of ACoA parenting. Developmentally speaking, there is nothing that trumps love, attention, and interaction.

Separating Our "Inner Child" from Our Children

ACoAs can be a curious combination of mature and immature parents. Having been parentified—that is having been little adults and caretakers as COAs—they can be unusually responsible about managing the nuts and bolts of parenting. But at the same time they may carry buried, developmental wounds that create immature "pockets" within their personalities and their functioning as parents that get triggered by their GCoA children. As GCoAs grow, they stimulate the unhealed wounds of their parents. For example, when the GCoA is five years old, the ACoA's "inner five-year-old" can be triggered, which means that if there is unhealed pain, it is felt by the ACoA. But they don't necessarily know why they feel as they do. And the ACoA's taboo against feeling their hidden pain gets activated. So at the same time as they are feeling vulnerable, out of control, or anxious, they are trying not to feel those things. Then that pain can get unconsciously projected, re-created, and reenacted in the parent/child relationship. The GCoAs "inherit" the unfelt and disowned pain of their ACoAs parents, which may in turn make them feel confused and bad about themselves. And they don't know why.

Serena, a client of mine, is an ACoA who has two young children of her own. In Serena's case, we see how, when ACoAs become parents, they can confuse their own unhealed CoA pain with the normal aches and pains of their children. This can make GCoAs feel that there is something inside of them that needs changing, something wrong with them that is worrying their parent.

> *I worried about my kids more than my other mom friends did. I was always looking at them too hard. I hated leaving them, even for a while. I worried while I wasn't there. I couldn't have fun and let go—I mean I could, sort of, sure, but something nagged at me. I was fearful. If some little friend rejected them, I wanted to crawl under the table and curl up in a little ball and cry. Or write the other kid a poison-pen letter. And I could get really mad really fast. I would be patient for a long time and then boom—right to big anger. And it freaked my kids out. I always apologized, but I did it again. And again. It's hard for me to set bound- aries and stick to them . . . I want my kids not to be . . . well, not to reject me, I guess.*

Serena was admitting to what felt like a lot of faults, she didn't realize how typical she was of an ACoA who was now a parent. She went on:

I wanted to join my children in their lighthearted fun, to laugh and play with them. But the truth is my heart was not light. My inner child had things to say and tears to cry. She wanted to shout and scream. And laugh and dance. And feel, I guess. It was like parts of me were just not . . . not really there. Like I wasn't living in my own skin that false self-functioning you talk about, I have some of that, I think.

I asked Serena if she wanted to choose someone to play the wounded child inside of her. ACOA parents often confuse the pain of the child they are raising (in this case, Lass) with the unresolved pain of their own "inner child"; they disown their inner pain and project it onto their child. Then they set about trying to "fix" in their child what really needs fixing inside of them. Sometimes it is useful to have chairs representing both and to talk to both so the ACOA can separate them. Serena began by speaking to her own "inner child." I then asked Serena to add an empty chair to represent her daughter Lass.

Serena to her inner child: *"I see you there all curled up, and I want to put a blanket over you so no one else can see you, so I can't see you really, you bother me, you seem so pathetic."*

Serena to Lass: *I get you mixed up with the child in me, Lass. Whenever you hurt, I think I need to protect you or fix you or distract you or something. I don't know how to just be with you.*

I get my feelings all mixed up with yours . . . it's a mess . . . then I want to shut it all down, make it go away.

I asked Serena what she would like to do next.

"I guess I'd like to talk with the child inside of me again, " said Serena.

Serena to her own inner child: *You aren't Lass, and it's not fair to Lass for you not to own your own pain. I know you don't want to, but I will help you. I will see you and try to listen to you and get the help we need to heal. I guess I need to listen to you so you will stop acting out your pain all over the place. I do want to know you.*

Serena turned to me. "I think I want to talk to Lass now," then she turned to the empty chair representing Lass.

Serena to Lass: *I love you so much, Lass, and I don't want you to have to have this on top of you, but I am so scared of losing you. I felt so—I don't know—extra, invisible . . . I don't know why, and I feel awful saying it, but I feel so good with you. Finally it feels like I have someone safe to love, someone who won't reject me. But, I get it: if I cling to you and am so possessive, I am setting it up so that one day you might need to push me away. I always thought it was because I didn't ever want you to feel rejected the way I was, but now I think it was because I don't want to feel rejected either.*

Serena stops for a moment and moves the chairs a few inches apart.

Serena to both Lass and her own inner child: *I never saw this before or even thought of it. You both look so much happier when you aren't on top of each other; I feel so much better when I am not on top of you, Lass. I am sorry, I really couldn't tell the difference between you as a child and my inner child; it was all mixed up inside of me. Your pain just triggered mine and then I swung into action, taking care of you so I didn't have to feel.. I'm sorry; what a burden for you to carry around. I get it . . . I get it. I see it—we're close, of course we're close, why wouldn't we be? This is always what I wanted with my mom, my dad, and we had it, sort of. We had it sometimes, but it was just so complicated. I don't want to be so complicated with you. I don't want to confuse little Serena's wounds with yours. She isn't you and you aren't her.*

This role-play allowed Serena to get a visual picture of separating her wounded inner child from her healthy, happy daughter. Serena runs the risk of creating pain that doesn't need to be there if she doesn't make this connection. The bonus here for Serena is that her love for her daughter will motivate her to do her own work because she truly does want to protect her daughter from pain. But now the light has dawned and Serena sees that she may be the cause of passing down pain unnecessarily and that the best thing she can do for her daughter is to heal her own wounded self. Protecting her daughter means getting help for herself.

In a different sort of example, another client named Robert describes how the dynamics of what was learned at one dinner table made its way straight to the next generation's dinner table. After several months of group work, Robert was developing an ability to have his eye on his own behavior.

"I don't know what happens to me," Robert admitted. "We'll

just be sitting at the dinner table and someone will ask me a question, and I am off to the races. I'm not even sure how much time passes. I just start giving advice and I can't stop."

"Where do you remember that happening at other times?" I asked.

"My father took over the dinner table. I could never open my mouth. He never asked me a question or seemed to realize that I was even there. He was a narcissist and an addict. It was awful. I was nobody. We were all nobodies."

"What would you have liked to say to your father in those moments?" I asked, pointing to an empty chair.

Robert to his father: "I'm here. I'm not invisible. I have things to say, too."

"Anything else?" I asked.

Robert's face darkened and he glared at the chair. "Can't you shut up? You're obnoxious; I feel like I can't stand this, like I have to make myself numb to stay here. This is horrible. I feel tied to this stupid chair, like I can't move."

Night after night at this dinner table had left Robert feeling erased and angry. And because he had never put these pieces together, he passed on the pain by "becoming" his father, doing to his wife and children what was done to him.

Pointing to another chair, I asked Robert to say what he wanted to say to the silenced and humiliated little boy inside of him.

Robert to his inner child: "I can't even look at you, you look so sad to me, even pathetic. Come on, come with me, I am going to take you out of here. You have been living in this chair all your life. It's time to get up."

In Robert's example, we see how his father's narcissism was passed along to his children. Even though Robert is himself not as narcissistic as his father, he has mirrored the same unattuned behaviors that he grew up with. His willingness to become aware of them and the emptiness that he feels inside as a result of re-creating them through psychodrama are wonderful first steps toward changing them and developing new relationship skills. Once he could feel the feelings he had in the past, the solution revealed itself naturally.

Robert to his inner child: "Get up, move, leave, you don't have to spend the rest of your life in that chair. You've grown up, you're a man now; get up and leave the table."

Breaking the Pain Chain

Who we are on the inside becomes what we do as parents. We cannot possibly read enough parenting books to undo the damaging effects of PTSD. We may gain a better intellectual understanding of what happened to us and that is vital, but we still need to feel our way back into the here and now, to revisit disparate parts of ourselves that have been partially banished from conscious awareness. No amount of well-intentioned "time outs" for our kids or "parenting tips" for us can match the useful-ness of getting the help we need to become healthier people so that we can be healthier partners and parents. We need to change on the inside.

Feeling unfelt childhood fear, pain, and anger can be

frightening and disequalibrating, but it is also very enlightening and relieving. It will be critical for Serena and Robert to, in a sense, reparent themselves so that they become different on the inside. Their adult self needs to step up to the plate and "take care of" their child self. ACoAs can be outward-focused; they are caretakers of others, but when it comes to their own needs, they may be less attuned.

Serena and Robert are revisiting their past roles so that they can reclaim and release themselves, and they may need to do this over and over again for a significant period of time. Trauma symptoms developed in ACoAs over a period of many years; ACoAs need to heal over a period of several years.

As an AcoA's personal work evolves, parenting will shift naturally. ACoA's need to "self-parent" as they parent. As we separate our own past from our own present process, make new meaning of and integrate parts of ourselves that may have been held out of conciousness, our inner boundaries become clearer and more distinct and our outer boundaries follow. Our parenting becomes cleaner; we can tell the difference between our wounded inner child and the child we have brought into the world.

Tips for ACoA Parents to Break the Pattern

- Find a middle ground. ACoAs don't know what normal is (Woititz 1983). As we have discussed throughout the book, ACoAs have trouble with modulation, and our parenting may tend to reflect this. I am not suggesting that we become bland, but rather that we simply hold ourselves to the kind of emotional balance that allows for normal levels of upset and frustration to rise to the surface and be felt and expressed but not blown out of proportion.

- Relax. Be aware of a tendency toward being hypervigilant in parenting. ACoA parents may "wait for the other shoe to drop" or "walk on egg shells" in the families we create; this is what we learned in childhood. But this is not helpful for our children, as it creates anxiety in them.

- Don't make your kids into your dysfunctional parents or siblings. Be aware of transferences and projections. Our children are sitting ducks when it comes to transferring our unresolved pain onto them. Our children can "remind" us of our own parents and siblings, and we may unwittingly assume that they possess qualities they do not possess because of it and project our associated pain onto them where it does not belong.

- Get help resolving your own historical issues. Our disowned, unspoken pain gets acted out through our attitudes, projections, and our behavior toward our children. Cleaning up our side of the street is one of the first things we should do if we feel locked in conflict with our kids or we see that our kids are picking up on our bad relationship habits and attitudes. If we are worried about our kids, we should take a good, hard look at ourselves to see what we might be "doing" or "being" that is affecting their behavior.

- Be aware of your triggers. What triggers us tells us where our vulnerabilities lie and where our personal pain might be. We need to be aware of what relationship dynamics or issues push our buttons so that we can back up and take a breath when they get pushed. We can make a "note to self" about what triggers us and what feelings come up when we're getting triggered so that we can process them at a calmer moment. In this way, our trigger points become grist for the mill in our personal growth and our growth as a parent.

- Create daily rituals and gatherings for holidays. ACoAs may have experienced interrupted or broken rituals as a result of living with addiction. But rituals are important; they affirm the bonds of life and relationship; they sink into our tapestry of memories and ground us in our families and with our friends. Consciously building healthy, happy rituals that feel manageable and enjoyable is an important part of parenting and living in a family. Reliable is more important than lavish; it is the getting together and affirming bonds that is important.

- Remember self-care. While taking care of others is a core feature of parenting, we need to take care of ourselves as a part of that process. Take breaks, have fun, relax, get exercise, and spend time with friends.

- Have fun, relax, and play with your kids. ACoAs can be what is known in the vernacular as "terminally serious." Play is bonding and tension relieving, and it teaches teamwork in an easy way. All species play; it is an integral way in which both human and animal babies build social skills. And relaxing with our kids builds trust and ease in the family. It sends a positive message to kids that home is where you can be yourself and be loved for who you are.

- Pass along what you love. Children absorb and model what they sense that their parents love. Whatever you love, whether taking walks, cooking, painting, music, sports, or taking a Sunday drive, share it with your kids. Many times these interests build themselves right into the personal or professional futures of our children. And they remember where they learned those interests; it is a way of feeling close to a parent for a child to be initiated into the inner sanctums of their parents' cherished activities.

- Have a good relationship with your child's other parent or stepparent. Who we are speaks louder that what we say. We are our children's models on how to live in an intimate relationship; we demonstrate reasonableness and getting along through our actions. We show what love looks like and how it feels and whether we are with our children's spouse or not, we owe them a respectful rapport with the parent with whom we chose to bring them into this world.

- Don't turn your children into little parents by making them confidantes. As ACoAs, we have a lot to get off our chests and a deep need to do so. Having perhaps felt at the disempowered end of a power imbalance with our own parent, we may share too much of our ACoA pain with our children with whom we may feel more empowered and trusting.

- Take time. There is no substitute for time: in this busy world we may forget that it is the time that we spend (or don't spend) with our children that they will remember. In Antoine de Saint-Exupéry *The Little Prince*, the title character recognizes that it is the time he "wastes" on his flower, on tending her, listening to her, and making sure that she has the attention she so desires, that makes the flower so special to him. " . . . in herself alone she is more important than all the hundreds of you other roses: because it is she that I have watered; because it is she that I have put under the glass globe; because it is she that I have sheltered behind the screen; because it is for her that I have killed the caterpillars (except the two or three that we saved to become butterflies); because it is she that I have listened to, when she grumbled, or boasted, or ever sometimes when she said nothing. Because she is my rose." So it is with children: it is the time that we fritter away together doing this and that, the feeling a child has knowing that his mother is in the next room or that his father's door is ajar while he plays that gives a deep sense that all is well, that family is good.

The Spiritual Journey of Parenting

There are few if any experiences in life that pull on our insides, warm up forgotten parts of ourselves, and move us to be better people than we ever thought we could be than parenting. We look into the faces of our children and we see little balls of our own DNA staring up at us, telling us by their very presence that life is good, that life goes on. These tiny creatures have the power to reach their little hands into our hearts and literally massage life into them or tug on their unhealed parts, or most often both.

We are, through our children, returned to our own childhood states. Therein lies the sacred opportunity to break the pattern of dysfunction and grow spiritually. When the pain comes up, do we process it and try to understand it or do we mindlessly reenact the past and pass down either what we got or its polar opposite? What gets triggered in the course of parenting offers us a window into our unconscious and our unmet developmental issues, gaps, needs, and strengths. The three-year-old we hold in our arms calls to the three-year-old in us, and we are brought toward a forgotten land, a forgotten self. The deep feelings that get triggered tell us where our inner work lies, and we are offered a second chance at living, at healing and restoring our own inner child.

As ACoAs we can use our experiences to become spiritually awakened because we have something called recovery. We see firsthand the importance of not being fake, of not living superficially. If we are willing to look at our own disease pattern and not just at our parents and our past, we can use our experiences to make ourselves humble, tender, and thoughtful parents as well as smart, creative, and independent adults.

SEVENTEEN

Mindfulness and the Gift of Trauma

Siddhartha looked into the flowing river.
Never had a river attracted him as much as this one.
Never had the voice and appearance of the flowing water
seemed so beautiful. It seemed that the river had something
special to tell him, Something which he did not know.

—*Siddhartha*

There is something in the river, something that draws us, that teaches and enlightens; that allows us to remember how transient all of life really is. A rippling reflection of ourselves and the world around us stares up at us from the water's flowing surface. For an instant, that transient image might be illumined by a shaft of sunlight or parting clouds, allowing us to glimpse what is normally not visible; to become aware of what was probably always there, but we were somehow not able to see. Something below the surface of our being that we "do not know" becomes known to us. A deeper layer of self becomes visible. And then it passes, dissolves, and becomes part of the rolling waters once again. And we have to keep traveling the river to expose its further secrets. We have to wait for more images to reveal themselves, to learn what we are meant to learn. We have to embark upon our own inner journey.

The gift of trauma is that it deepens us layer by layer. It pushes us to our psychological, emotional, and spiritual limits and teaches us to hold more emotion than we are used to holding, to see more than we are used to seeing, to contain, observe, and look for meaning.

All people get hurt; pain is part of being alive and in a body. In the same way that we will have body bruises and broken bones, we will have emotional wounds and broken hearts. But we have a choice as to what we do with what happens to us. The art of life, as the saying goes, "is to play the hand we're dealt" as well as we can.

Our thinking mind is one of human beings' most dazzling gifts. With it, we can make sense of our own experience. It is through our thinking mind that we can imagine something as abstract as a sense of self and reflect on ourselves in relationship to our world. This is how man made fire, airplanes, music, art, the computer, and how we structure something as conceptual as a consciousness of past and future.

But even with all of this evolutionary distinction, our intellect is still only an instrument in our living hands, because our direct experience of life happens in the present moment, not in our heads.

Relationship of the Thinking Mind to the Body/Mind

If we watch our own hand pick up a spoon and bring it to our mouth, we see what a seamless and amazing machine the body/mind is as it executes this incredibly complicated task. Our senses guide us as the spoon moves and finds its placement through space. If we think at all, it may be just to watch the picture of our arm as it passes before our eyes, or to wonder about how our food will taste.

But usually, we are nowhere near this experience. Usually we are a million miles away as we mindlessly bring the spoon up to our mouth again and again and eat without tasting. We are somewhere else. Our intellect is not doing this lovely job of being still and observing, maybe having a thought or two about what is going on in the here and now to enhance our feeling of being present. Rather our intellect is leaping around, taking us far away from the moment, probably somewhere in the future or in the past. Most of us spend the bulk of our time just like this. Somewhere else.

Returning to the Present. Trauma essentially takes us out of our present moment. When something is happening that is overwhelming us, the moment gets too painful to stay in. So we become defensive; we find some way to remove ourselves from the present. We build large, defensive structures, essentially designed to ward off what is happening that we can't handle. Though emotionally fleeing from the moment can provide a temporary safe haven, it can have long-term effects that undermine our ability to be present to our own inner and outer worlds.

Healing trauma is a process of returning to the here and now, of unpacking our defenses so that we can feel what went unfelt, understand the significance of what we're feeling in terms of our self structure, and reintegrate what have been heretofore disintegrated, unprocessed pieces of experience. We need to own all of who we are so that we can feel whole. Resolving the frozenness of trauma allows us to feel more alive in the present.

Pain Templates

We template our early experiences, and those templates become a baseline from which we operate. What we do when our templates from the past get triggered defines a critical moment. Do we use what is getting triggered as fodder for personal growth, or do we just pass on pain? Do we project our pain outward, disowning it in ourselves, thus throwing an old template onto a new experience? Or do we recognize that a pain template from the past is getting triggered in the present and is being layered upon and mixed in with the situation we're in right now—that we're about to re-create an old pattern in a new circumstance?

Self-Sabotaging. Psychologist Peter Levine speaks about triggers in terms of energy and the ability of a threat to literally overwhelm the activating systems of the brain. When we are traumatized, for example, if the energy from the threat that is occurring is not discharged successfully at the actual moment that the threat is happening, along with its accompanying feelings and behaviors, the traumatic moment becomes imprinted in the brain. Then, each time this moment of threat is triggered by some cue in the present that is reminiscent of the original hurt, the body goes into its "defensive position." Each time we respond to a perceived threat, first biochemically and then behaviorally with actions designed to minimize this threat, a "blueprint" of attempted survival strategies is re-created and stored in both the body and the brain and we, in a sense, retraumatize ourselves (Levine 2004).

Emotional Whiplash. Someone who is rear-ended in a car is taken by surprise. In a millisecond the body reaches out to defend itself; often throwing out an arm and the head goes suddenly forward and back in movements that are outside of its normal range of motion. In whiplash, the neck muscles can freeze in that position in a thwarted action of self-defense. The large muscles are stretched beyond capacity and weakened, and the small ones go into trauma trying to support what the large ones can no longer support. And each time there is the threat of further harm, those now-kindled and sensitive nerve endings react all over again as if the threat were as real as it was the first time. The muscles are caught in a cycle in which they retraumatize themselves. Healing whiplash requires those muscles to release that thwarted movement and complete it with awareness and/ or to be "taught" how to regain their more normal patterns of movement, in order to rebuild their strength and resilience.

There is such a thing as emotional whiplash—when our emotional muscles get overstretched and our sustaining core is weakened. Then we try to use defenses like denial, minimization, repression, or intellectualization, to shore ourselves up, because our core emotional muscles are traumatized. And they get oversensitized, so that every time there is a signal that we may be hurt, we throw out a new blueprint of the old relationship dynamic and re-create and deepen that pattern—in a sense, retraumatizing ourselves.

One common way that this passing down of pain from past to present can occur in our relationships is through a dynamic that psychoanalysts call *projective identification*, in which we project qualities—good or bad—on another person that match up with what we already have experienced, and we behave in such a way as to elicit responses in that other person that match up with our existing templates or blueprints. In other words we draw out of them the very behavior we fear most. Our minds tend to perceive selectively; we give less attention to qualities that do not match up with our templates and more to those that do. We look for qualities of rejection or subterfuge that match up with what we may have known, and we expect or even elicit them from the people we're relating to, convinced that what we see is all there is. Or we can assume that people will feel positively toward us. In other words, we elicit what we assume is there. In either case, we behave according to our template.

The Gift of Awareness and Self-Reflection

When we are triggered, which is inevitable, we need to learn new strategies for feeling management Expecting life to have bumps and having tools to deal with them can actually help us use moments of being triggered to grow from rather than retraumatize ourselves. When we're triggered, simply breathing through pain, allowing our perceptions of threat to ease and doing something different from the old pattern can work wonders. A small change in our knee-jerk reaction can interrupt the template and open the door for change and growth. We can quiet our minds and our reactions so that we can observe and understand where something that is happening on the outside might be sending us on the inside. When we do this, we can use moments of being triggered as moments of healing; because what triggers us most is often what has hurt us most; it sends a signal up from where our deep, unconscious pain lies. If there was not unresolved pain there, we would not feel so vulnerable; our reactions would be less intense.

Life is a constant process of injury and repair. Recovery allows us to rework moments from the past that have us stuck in our present so we can release ourselves from an endless and self-perpetuating cycle of stubbornly reenacting and re-creating old templates of experience—so we can become more relaxed, porous, and open to new experience.

The Gift of Presence in the Present

Self-awareness and self-reflection are what allow us to live life consciously, to see ourselves in action, witness the workings of our own inner being, and observe and understand others. In order to calmly self-reflect, we need to be able to be in a state of mind that is not distracted. Following the breath as it moves in and out of us is an age-old method of connecting our mind and body, calming down our nervous system, and reducing racing thoughts.

Thich Nhat Hanh, nominated for the Nobel Peace Prize and author of *The Miracle of Mindfulness*, says:

Simply breathe in mindfully and bring your mind home to your body, and when your breath is home in the body you are in the here and now, in the present. Follow your breath with awareness from beginning to end . . . By doing this we cultivate concentration . . . and through concentration, we cultivate insight . . . and insight is a miracle, we just breathe in, and we touch the miracle of being alive. Breathing in we become aware of our body . . . we may notice tension and pain we have allowed to accumulate. We have not treated our body tenderly; we can always allow tension to be released by breathing in mindfully, by breathing out mindfully.

Nhat Hanh tells us that through these simple practices we can learn how to recognize a feeling of joy and generate a feeling of happiness within ourselves: "In order to generate joy, you come home to your body and you come home to the here and now and you recognize that there are so many conditions of happiness that are only available in the here and now."

Only You Really Know

Only we know where it hurts and how much. No therapist, however talented, can know exactly where or how much we're feeling pain; we barely know it ourselves. No system can rescue us if we don't allow ourselves to be helped. No diagnostician can help us if we don't talk about what is going on inside of us. We know the intricacies of our inner world, where we love and care the most, where our pain is sharp, dull, or like emotional pinpricks. Where we have no feeling at all.

In the same way that we need to take charge of our physical health, we need to stay on top of our mental health. We need to develop a language and a context for healing. Part of healing is finding good help, and the other parts are developing a self-help Rolodex and building skills of emotional processing. We need to know where to go to get help when we need it and how to manage and process our feelings and thoughts as they are occurring. Once we learn to read our own symptoms and triggers and understand the basics of transference, projection, and reenactment dynamics, we're in a position to be our own first line of defense. And we have a better sense of when to seek help and what kind of help to seek. Our personal prescription may be just a day off or a spa day; it might be time with a friend, a hobby, a family member, or nature; or we might need to seek out a 12-step program, a therapist, or treatment. The more we learn, the more our adult self is in a position to make good decisions and choices.

thening the Compassionate Inner Adult

s a stage in recovery where we really just want to let our child speak with absolutely no thought of what another person might feel like at hearing it. One might say that this is, in a way, a correction for all of the times we fell silent or felt erased. Part of finding that frozen self is giving our inner child full rein to feel and speak. That's the part of recovery from ACoA issues that is serious family-of-origin work. When we first unthaw our frozen inner child, adolescent, or young adult, the floodgates open, and all the withheld emotion comes pouring forward. And that is right for that time. But eventually, as with any child, inner or outer, we need to grow up, we need to learn the skills of effective communication, and we need to realize that no matter how strongly we feel, other's feelings need to be taken into account as well. ACoAs and codependents have often put the feelings of others before their own, at great personal expense. In recovery, the child within finds a voice, and so does the inner adolescent, young adult, and so on—the silenced selves come forward.

But ACoAs also need to find their inner adult. Too often we talk to the world from our wounded inner child and then we're disappointed when no one hears us clearly. If we cannot hold our own inner child because we find our anxiety and pain overwhelming, why do we think someone else should be able to? We blurt out our unedited pain and anger, then we feel hurt, misunderstood, and disappointed all over again when the other person does not want to hear it.

The first person who needs to hold and listen to our inner

child is us. Our inner child needs to open up to our inner adult, and our adult self needs to hold our hurting self as we would hold a crying child—with caring and compassion. We need to simply breathe with, love, and hold the child within us; we need to care. Then our adult self needs to translate what our child is trying to say into adult language that can be effectively communicated to someone else.

When we allow our inner child to blurt out each and every reaction before the adult in us makes any attempt to understand, hold, and translate feelings into words so they can be lifted into conscious and intelligent thought, we sabotage ourselves and our relationships. We don't communicate in a way that others can understand, and we don't take that other person into consideration. What we do when we are triggered will have much to do with whether or not we re-create past pain in the present.

The Dark Kaleidoscope of Trauma

Along with the capacity to imagine a future and make plans for it, to invent and imagine, our thinking mind can create endless, dark scenarios that make us want to retreat from life. Years of repressing and denying our pain and giving into the will of others can make us feel we should ignore nothing, that we have to dissect every random thought or feeling that we have and stand up for

so strongly that we become stubborn and inf

But that's not normal. Though long-term

constant work, care, and maintenance, they

emergency room all the time, and we needn't be there either. Remember, the same medicine we need in a crisis or to cure infection can become poison in healthy conditions or in too high a dose. The body may need heroics to deal with a disease or set a bone, but then it needs time to heal and rehab. And eventually, it will just need healthy care and maintenance.

So it is with the mind. Resolving old feelings may require us to delve and dissect, but living day to day may call for additional skill sets. We need to learn when to pay attention and when to let go, when to act and when to just breathe. Sometimes all we need to do is tolerate our painful feelings and comfort ourselves so we don't behave in such a way as to make everything worse than it is.

Sometimes talking is enough. The spoken word is an action. It is the end result of a complex process of feeling, owning, and translating emotions and thoughts into language. And it's the beginning of communication through words. It is first intrapersonal and then interpersonal.

Therapy and pop psychology might erroneously give the impression that there is an ultimate goal, a place to arrive where we will finally be whole, intact, and cured; that there is some sort of "there" to get to, that there is such a thing as being healed once and for all. But the self is a flexible and fluid construction in a perpetual cycle of renewal and repair. We are constantly dealing with and healing from the slings and arrows of life. What we want to achieve is the ability to operate within a healthy range, where the self can be repeatedly injured and heal from injury, like the body. This is why we build physical, emotional, psychological, and spiritual resilience, so we can stay fit for life.

But we are always a self in motion, a self in an evolving sense of relationship. A self constantly experimenting with and developing a new relationship with its own core values and the values of the world it experiences. Our self is always evolving in relationship to others and in how we interact, listen, share, and co-create a relational space. A healthy sense of self can adapt, ever modifying itself, establishing and reestablishing its own equilibrium within the inevitable and perpetual fluctuations of life.

Hurt Isn't Broken: Reframing

To watch someone you love lose themselves a little more each day and become someone you hardly recognize is an unforgettable experience. To witness as they become someone who they hate themselves for being but cannot stop being and you hate what they have become but still love them is life altering. Living with the disease of addiction changes everyone. It affects us in both good and not so good ways. And then we have a choice. Do we pass on the pain we experienced to future generations, or do we do the best we can to break the chain of pain in our generation? Do we become bitter about life and relationships, or do we find a way to hold this experience and allow it to make us deeper and wiser?

One of our great capacities as evolving humans is turning weaknesses into strengths. If, for example, you learned ~ ACoA that you could not depend on anyone, you ~

that you don't wait around and hope that others will hand you a life—you go out and create one for yourself. Or if you had to assume managerial roles in your family that deprived you of some of your youth, the upside is that you developed management skills at a time in your life when you simply had to use what was at hand and get things to work—before adult fears set in and told you that what you were doing was something you shouldn't even think of trying. If there was little food in the house to cook dinner with, you learned to be creative and ingenious with what you had. If age-appropriate toys were lacking, you made up your own games. ACoAs learn to be creative and to take risks because we have to, and that creativity and risk-taking can and often does serve us well as adults.

Another lesson: you can lose the people you love. The upside is that we don't take love for granted, and we know that good relationships can be ruined if we don't take care of them. We learned that the people we loved, both good and kind, could fall apart. And so can we. So we turn that one around and get good at self-care, and we become willing to honestly confront issues that may undermine personal and interpersonal health and happiness, because we know that in the long run it will be better. And we learn to appreciate life and people while we have them; we know that nothing, good or bad, lasts forever.

It's important to look around us: people go through horrible things, much worse things than we can imagine or have probably gone through ourselves. If we're going to "compare and despair," we should also compare and be grateful, because we have recovery when so many others don't. There is something soothing, purifying, and humbling in processing pain that allows us to emerge more free and whole and alive. Something that puts us in touch with a side of life that we normally skate over; something that grows soul and expands our capacity to be spiritually alive and present to the mystery and moment of life.

One of the gifts of trauma for many ACoAs like me is that it brings 12-step programs into our lives. I will always have these words from the Alanon greeting burned into my heart: "You may not love all of us, but you will come to love us in a very special way, the same way that we already love you. Talk with each other, reason things out but let there be no gossip . . . let the understanding and peace of the program grow in you a day at a time." These words held me when I needed holding. There was more spiritual sunlight and emotional and psychological fresh air in those dusty back rooms and basements than I can explain. Initially, I was simply glad to share what I really felt and not clear the room out. To say what was in my heart and have nothing around me explode. In fact, nothing happened at all. People said things like, "Thanks for sharing" or "me, too." It changed my life.

"You will not regret nor wish to close the door on the past." Another promise of the program that came true. Alanon gave me a wonderful sense of being connected to a reliable, easily accessible community, one that was based on "principles not personalities." Now when I look back, I find love, strength, beauty, and pictures in my mind of people doing their best. I feel I had a great beginning, that I was just where I was meant to be.

In early recovery we need to create a strong enough support system to help to hold our outpouring of pain, which can include

12-step programs, group therapy, and one-to-one therapy. We need a strong enough container of care to hold us during the mysterious and deepening experience of getting to know ourselves on the inside.

Then comes the long-term maintenance, the self-care, and self-repair. Our relationships are a sustaining part of our lives that need constant maintenance, and families are always going through new stages of life that come with their own challenges.

Coming Home: The Gift of Integration

We cannot heal what we don't feel. When in the course of resolving trauma we "reenter" our bodies and actually feel the emotions that we split off in a moment of fear, imagery follows. Colors, shapes, and moments of forgotten time come into view as pieces of the puzzle of us; fall together, sometimes gently and sometimes not so gently. And we have a curious sense of déjà vu, of having lived them before; as if someone we have known well and forgotten is being remembered.

That someone is ourselves. We're integrating what was fragmented, mending what was torn, and increasing our capacity to feel whole, alive, and present.

Our physician lies within. Good therapy helps us to get in touch with, educate, and strengthen our own internal healer. It allows us to learn to depend in healthy ways so that we become capable of close relationships. It strengthens our autonomy. Recovery is a journey of personal and interpersonal expansion that we are in charge of, one that can and often does include a spiritual awakening. In developing the awareness to mine our own depths and bring our shadow selves into the light of awareness, we actually deepen our capacity for being in the moment.

People in my groups who have been in long-term recovery report something curious: though they continue to have problems in life, they no longer experience those problems as traumatic in the way that they did before they had awareness and tools and strategies for coping. They do not expect life to be problem-free, and they have equipped themselves for processing the pain they are in while they are actually in it. They aren't freezing up and storing it in the body or splitting it off and throwing it out of consciousness. They are living in the present. They stop asking "When will I finally get there?" because they realize that there is no "there." That life is simply appreciating the moment, the now, that the whole idea is to strengthen their inner being enough so they can enjoy the ride, so they can live this thing called life.

Invariably, when groups do psychodrama, pain comes up and out as they boldly "take the stage" or inhabit their own personal role. What they did not get to say as a helpless child is said, what they did not get to do is done, and what they did not feel is felt. The silent scream is no longer silent. And then the joy of self-discovery somehow takes over and they are in touch with their inner being. They see the whole situation in a new and more personally meaningful light, they decathect from a moment in time that had them ensnared in its unconscious grip. And they smile, they laugh, and their body and face move more freely. They have expanded their range of emotional motion.

As Sandy put it one evening when he was going through the closure of his good-byes and moving on from group: "I saw you do your psychodrama tonight. I saw you struggle to let yourself feel, to let yourself say what you wanted to say. I saw you start to feel. It was like a door inside you opened up. I remembered that moment when I started group and had that feeling. When it came to me . . . when that door . . . I mean, I had been waiting so long for something to happen . . . when that door inside me opened and I finally realized . . . I saw . . . that the person who was holding it closed all along, was me."

References

Ackerman, R. J. 1989. *Perfect Daughters*. Deerfield Beach, FL: Health Communications.

Adams, C. E., F. L. Greenway, and P. J. Brantley. 2011. "Lifestyle Factors and Ghrelin: Critical Review and Implications for Weight Loss Maintenance." *Obesity Review* 12(5): e211–e218, electronic publication.

Ahnert, L., M. R. Gunnar, M. E. Lamb, and M. Barthel. 2004. "Transition to Child Care: Associations with Infant-Mother Attachment, Infant Negative Emotion, and Cortisol Elevations." *Child Development* 75(3):649–650.

Anda, R. F., V. J. Felitti, J. Walker, C. L. Whitfield, J. D. Bremner, B. D. Perry, S. R. Dube, and W. H. Giles. 2006. "The Enduring Effects of Abuse and Related Adverse Experiences in Childhood: A Convergence of Evidence from Neurobiology and Epidemiology." *European Archives of Psychiatry and Clinical Neurosciences* 256(3):174–86.

Anda, R. F., V. J. Felitti, D. W. Brown, D. Chapman, M. Dong, S. R. Dube, V. I. Edwards, and W. H. Giles. 2006. "Insights into Intimate Partner Violence from the Adverse Childhood Experiences (ACE) Study." In P. R. Salber and E. Taliaferro, eds., *Physician's Guide to Intimate Partner Violence and Abuse*, Volcano, CA: Volcano Press.

American Psychiatric Association. *Diagnostic and Statistical Manual of Mental Disorders*, fourth edition. 1994. Washington, DC: American Psychiatric Association.

Badenoch, B. 2008. *Being a Brain-Wise Therapist: A Practical Guide to Interpersonal Neurobiology*. New York: W. W. Norton.

Beesley, D. and C. D. Stoltenberg. 2002. "Control, Attachment Style, and Relationship Satisfaction Among Adult Children of Alcoholics." *Journal of Mental Health Counseling* 24(4): 281–298.

Black, C. 1981 (ACT); 1987. *It Will Never Happen to Me! Children of Alcoholics: As Youngsters—Adolescents—Adults*. New York: Ballantine Books.

————. 1982. *Double Duty: Help for the Adult Child.* Deerfield Beach, FL: Health Communications.

Blumenthal, J. A., M. A. Babyak, K. A. Moore, W. E. Craighead, S. Herman, P. Khatri, R. Waugh, et al 1999. "Effects of Exercise Training on Older Patients with Major Depression." *Archives of Internal Medicine* 159:2349–2356.

Bonell-Pascual, E., S. Huline-Dickens, S. Hollins, S., et al. 1999. "Bereavement and Grief in Adults with Learning Disabilities. A Follow-up Study." *British Journal of Psychiatry* 175; 348–350.

Bowlby, J. 1969. *Attachment and Loss.* Vol. 1, Attachment. London: Hogarth Press; New York: Basic Books.

Bradshaw, J. 1988. *Healing the Shame that Binds You.* Deerfield Beach, FL: Health Communications.

Brazy, J. E. 1988. "Effects of Crying on Cerebral Blood Volume and Cytochrome aa3." *Journal of Pediatrics* 112(3)457–461.

Brizendine, L. 2006. *The Female Brain.* New York: Three Rivers Press

Brown, S. 1988. *Treating Adult Children of Alcoholics: A Developmental Perspective.* New York: Wiley.

Butler, S. R, M. R. Suskind, and S. M. Schanberg. 1978. "Maternal Behavior as a Regulator of Polyamine Biosynthesis in Brain and Heart of Developing Rat Pups." *Science* 199:445–447.

Carnes, P. 1997. *The Betrayal Bond: Breaking Free of Exploitive Relationships.* Deerfield Beach, FL: Health Communications.

Carpiano, R. M. 2012. "Sense of Community-belonging and Health Behaviour Change in Canada." *Journal of Epidemiology and Community Health* 66: 277–283. DOI: 10.1136/jech.2009.10356.

Cermak, T. L. and S. Brown. 1982. "Interactional Group Therapy with Adult Children of Alcoholics." *International Journal of Group Psychotherapy* 30:375–389.

Cermack, T. L. 1985. *A Primer on Adult Children of Alcoholics.* Deerfield Beach, FL: Health Communications.

Coe, C. L., et al. "Endocrine and Immune Responses to Separation and Maternal Loss in Non-Human Primates." Pages 163–199 in M. Reite and

T. Fields (Eds.), *The Psychology of Attachment and Separation*. New York: Academic Press.

Coyle, J. P., T. Nochajski, E. Maguin, A. Safyer, D. DeWit, and S. Macdonald. 2006. "An Exploratory Study of the Nature of Family Resilience in Families Affected by Parental Alcohol Abuse." *Journal of Family Issues* 10(12):1606–1623.

Cozolino, L. 2006. *The Neuroscience of Human Relationships*. New York: W. W. Norton.

Crawford, E., M. O. Wright, and A. Masten. 2005. "Resilience and Spirituality in Youth." Pages 355–370 in E. C. Roehlkepartain, P. E. King, L. Wagener, and P. L. Benson (Eds.), *Handbook of Spiritual Development in Childhood and Adolescence*. Thousand Oaks, CA: Sage.

Dayton, A. 2012. "Awareness = Prevention." Freedom Institute, April 13, 2012. Retrieved from http://www.freedominstitute.org/blog/addiction-and-recovery/awareness-prevention/.

Dayton, T. 2000. *Trauma and Addiction*. Deerfield Beach, FL: Health Communications.

———. 2005. *The Living Stage: A Step by Step Guide to Psychodrama, Sociometry, and Experiential Group Therapy*. Deerfield Beach, FL: Health Communications.

———. 2007. *Emotional Sobriety: From Relationship Trauma to Resilience and Balance*. Deerfield Beach, FL: Health Communications.

Dossey, Larry. 1993. *Healing Words: The Power of Prayer and the Practice of Medicine*. New York: HarperCollins.

Dube, S. R., J. W. Miller, D. W. Brown, W. H. Giles, V. J. Felitti, M. Dong, et al. 2006. "Adverse Childhood Experiences and the Association with Ever Using Alcohol and Initiating Alcohol Use During Adolescence." *Journal of Adolescent Health* 38(4):444.e1–444.e10.

Eisenberger, N.I., M. D. Lieberman, K. D. Williams. 2003. "Does Rejection Hurt? An fMRI Study of Social Exclusion." *Science* 302(5643): 290–292.

Ebersole, P. and K. L. De Vogler. 1981. "Meaning in Life: Category Self-Ratings." *Journal of Psychology* 107:289–293.

El-Guebaly, N., M. West, E. Maticka-Tyndale, and M. Pool. 1993. "Attachment among Adult Children of Alcoholics." *Addiction* 88:1405–1411.

Eth, S. and R. S. Pynoos (Eds.). 1985. *Post-Traumatic Stress Disorder in Children*. Washington, DC: American Psychiatric Publishing.

Fredrickson, B. 2009. *Positivity: Groundbreaking Research Reveals How to Embrace the Hidden Strength of Positive Emotions, Overcome Negativity, and Thrive*. New York: Three Rivers Press.

Freud, S. 1922. *Beyond the Pleasure Principle*. London: International Psycho-Analytical Press.

Klein, R. M. 1999. "The Hebb Legacy." *Canadian Journal of Experimental Psychology* 53(1):1–3. DOI: 10.1037/h0087295.

Klein, M. 1932. *The Psychoanalysis of Children*, A. Strachey translation. London: Hogarth Press.

Gigerenzer, G. 2007. *Gut Feelings: The Intelligence of the Unconscious*. New York: Viking.

Greenspan, S. 2000. *Building Healthy Minds: The Six Experiences that Create Intelligence And Emotional Growth in Babies and Young Children*. Boston: Da Capo Press.

Gunnar, M., L. Brodersen, M. Nachmias, K. Buss, J. Rigatuso. 1996. "Stress Reactivity and Attachment Security." *Dev Psychobiol* 29(3): 191–204.

Gunnar, M. 1998. "Quality of Care and Buffering of Neuroendocrine Stress Reactions: Potential Effects on the Developing Human Brain." *Prev Med* 27(2): 208–11.

Hagedorn, W. B. 2009. "The Call for a New Diagnostic and Statistical Manual of Mental Disorders Diagnosis: Addictive Disorders." *Journal of Addictions & Offender Counseling* 29:110–127.

Herman, J. L. 1992. *Trauma and Recovery*. New York: Basic Books.

Heron, P. 1994. "Non-Reactive Cosleeping and Child Behavior: Getting a Good Night's Sleep All Night, Every Night." Master's thesis, Department of Psychology, University of Bristol.

Hoebel, B. G., N. M. Avena, and P. Rada. 2009. "Sugar Versus Fat Bingeing: Notable Differences in Addictive-like Behaviors." *The Journal of Nutrition* 139(3): 623–625 doi: 10.3945/ jn.108.097584

Horney, K. 1950. *Neurosis and Human Growth*. New York: W. W. Norton.

Hofer, M. and H. Shair. 1982. "Control of Sleep-Wake States in the Infant Rat by Features of the Mother-Infant Relationship." *Developmental Psychobiology* 15: 229–243.

Hofer, M. 1983. "The Mother-Infant Interaction as a Regulator of Infant Physiology and Behavior." In L. Rosenblum and H. Moltz (Eds.), *Symbiosis in Parent-Offspring Interactions*. New York: Plenum.

Hollenbeck, A. R., E. J. Susman, E. D. Nannis, B. E. Strope, S. P. Hersh, A. S. Levine, and P. A. Pizzo. 1980. "Children with Serious Illness: Behavioral Correlates of Separation and Solution." *Child Psychiatry and Human Development* 11(1): 3–11.

Hollins, S., and V. Sinason. 2000. "Psychotherapy, Learning Disabilities and Trauma: New Perspectives." *British Journal of Psychiatry* 176: 32–36.

House, J. S., K. R. Landis, and D. Umberson. 1988. "Social Relationships and Health." *Science* 241(4865):540–545. DOI: 10.1126/science.3399889.

Janov, Arthur. 2000. *The Biology of Love*. Amherst, NY: Prometheus Books.

Johnson, A. A. 2002. "Want Better Grades? Go to Church." *Christianity Today* 46(6).

Johnson, P. M. and P. Kenny. 2010. "Addiction-like Reward Dysfunction and Compulsive Eating in Obese Rats: Role for Dopamine D2 Receptors" *Nature Neuroscience* 13(5): 635–41. DOI:10.1038/nn.2519. PMC 2947358. PMID 20348917.

Jordan, B. K., C. R. Marmar, J. A. Fairbank, W. E. Schlenger, R. A. Kulka, R. L. Hough et al. 1992. "Problems in Families of Male Vietnam Veterans with Posttraumatic Stress Disorder." *Journal of Consulting and Clinical Psychology* 60: 9169–26.

Jordan, B. K., W. E. Schlenger, R. L. Hough, R. A. Kulka, D. S. Weiss, J. A. Fairbank et al. 1991. "Lifetime and Current Prevalence of Specific Psychiatric Disorders among Vietnam Veterans and Controls. *Archives of General Psychiatry*, 48: 207–215.

Karr-Morse, R., and M. Wiley. 1998. From an interview with Dr. Allan Schore as cited in *Ghosts From the Nursery: Tracing the Roots of Violence*. New York: Atlantic Monthly Press.

Kaufman, J. and D. Charney. 2001. "Effects of Early Stress on Brain Structure and Function: Implications for Understanding the Relationship Between Child Maltreatment and Depression." *Developmental Psychopathology* 13(3): 451–471.

King, D. W., L. A. King, J. A. Fairbank, T. M. Keane, and G. Adams. 1998.

"Resilience-recovery Factors in Posttraumatic Stress Disorder among Female and Male Vietnam Veterans: Hardiness, Postwar Social Support, and Additional Stressful Life Events." *Journal of Personality and Social Psychology* 74: 420–434.

King, D. W., L. A. King, D. W. Foy, and D. M. Gudanowski. 1996. "Prewar Factors in Combat-related Posttraumatic Stress Disorder: Structural Equation Modeling with a National Sample of Female and Male Vietnam Veterans." *Journal of Consulting and Clinical Psychology* 64: 520–531.

King, D. W., L. A. King, D. W. Foy, T. M. Keane, and J. A. Fairbank. 1999. Posttraumatic Stress Disorder in a National Sample of Female and Male Vietnam Veterans: Risk Factors, War-zone Stressors, and Resilience-recovery Variables." *Journal of Abnormal Psychology* 108: 164–170.

King, D. W., L. A. King, D. M. Gudanowski, and D. L. Vreven. 1995. "Alternative Representations of War Zone Stressors: Relationships to Posttraumatic Stress Disorder in Male and Female Vietnam Veterans." *Journal of Abnormal Psychology* 104: 184–196.

Krystal, H. (Ed.). 1968. *Massive Psychic Trauma*. Madison, CT: International Universities Press.

———. 1978. "Trauma and Affects." *Psychoanalytic Study of the Child* 33:81–116.

Kuhn, C. M., S. R. Butler, and S. M. Schanberg. 1978. "Selective Depression of Serum Growth Hormone During Maternal Deprivation in Rat Pups." *Science* 201:1035–1036.

Kulka, R. A., W. E. Schlenger, J. A. Fairbank, R. L. Hough, B. K. Jordan, C. R. Marmar et al. 1990a. *The National Vietnam Veterans Readjustment Study: Tables of findings and technical appendices*. New York: Brunner/Mazel.

——-1990b. *Trauma and the Vietnam War Generation: Report of Findings from the National Vietnam Veterans Readjustment Study*. New York: Brunner/Mazel.

Laub, D., and N. C. Auerhahn. 1993. "Knowing and Not Knowing Massive Psychic Trauma: Forms of Traumatic Memory." *International Journal of PsychoAnalysis* 74: 287–302

Leath, C. 1999. "The Experience of Meaning in Life from a Psychological Perspective." Junior Paper, Psychology Honors Program, University of Washington, Seattle. http://purl.oclc.org/net/cleath/writings/meaning.htm.

Ledoux, J. 1996. *The Emotional Brain*. New York: Simon and Schuster.

Lehrer, J. 2009. *How We Decide*. Boston: Houghton Mifflin Harcourt.

Leiberman, A. F., and H. Zeanah. 1995. "Disorders of Attachment in Infancy." *Infant Psychiatry* 4: 571–587.

Lewis, T., F. Amini, and R. Lannon. 2000; 2001. *A General Theory of Love*. New York: Random House: Vintage.

Lifton, R. J. 1968. *Death in Life: Survivors of Hiroshima*. New York: Random House.

Ludington-Hoe, S. M., X. Cong, and F. Hashemi. 2002. "Infant Crying: Nature, Physiologic Consequences, and Select Intervention." *Neonatal Network* 21(2): 29–36.

Luthar, S. S. 2006. "Resilience in Development: A Synthesis of Research Across Five Decades." In D. Cicchetti and D. J. Cohen (Eds.), *Developmental Psychopathology: Risk, Disorder, and Adaptation*, second edition. New York: Wiley.

Manzoni G. M., F. Pagnini, A. Gorini, A. Preziosa, G. Castelnuovo, E. Molinari, and G. Riva. 2009. "Can Relaxation Training Reduce Emotional Eating in Women with Obesity? An Exploratory Study with 3 Months of Follow-Up." *Journal of the American Dietetic Association* 109(8): 1427–32.

Mathes, W. F., K. A. Brownley, M. D. Xiaofei Mo, and C. M. Bulik. 2009. "The Biology of Binge Eating." *Appetite* 52(3): 545–53.

MacPherson, M., L. Smith-Lovin, and M. E. Brashears. 2006. "Social Isolation in America: Changes in Core Discussion Networks over Two Decades." *American Sociological Review* 71(3): 353–375. doi: 10.1177/000312240607100301.

Middelton-Moz, J., and Dwinell, L. 1986. *After the Tears: Reclaiming the Personal Losses of Childhood*. Health Communications: Deerfield Beach, FL.

Moreno, J. L. 1953. *Who Shall Survive: Foundations of Sociometry, Group Psychotherapy and Psychodrama*. Beacon, NY: Beacon House.

———. 1964. *Psychodrama: Foundations of Psychotherapy*. Beacon, NY: Beacon House.

Nachmias, M., M. Gunnar, S. Mangelsdorf, R. H. Parritz, K. Buss. 1996. "Behavioral Inhibition and Stress Reactivity: The Moderating Role of Attachment Security." *Child Dev* 67(2): 508–22.

Nhat Hanh, T. 1975; 1976; 1999. *The Miracle of Mindfulness.* Boston: Beacon Press.

Otto, M., and J. M. J. Smits. 2011. *Exercise for Mood and Anxiety: Proven Strategies for Overcoming Depression and Enhancing Well-Being.* New York: Oxford University Press.

Panksepp J. B. 2003. "Feeling the Pain of Social Loss." *Science.* 302(5643): 237-239

Peterson, C., S. F. Maier, and M. E. P. Seligman. 1995. *Learned Helplessness: A Theory for the Age of Personal Control.* New York: Oxford University Press.

Pennebaker, J. W. 1997. *Opening Up: The Healing Power of Expressing Emotions.* New York: The Guilford Press.

Perry, B. D. 1997. "Incubated in Terror: Neurodevelopmental Factors in the 'Cycle of Violence'." In J. Osofsky (Ed.), *Children, Youth and Violence: The Search for Solutions.* New York: Guilford Press.

Pert, C. 1997. *Molecules of Emotion: The Science Behind Mind-Body Medicine.* New York: Simon & Schuster.

Putnam, F. W. 1985. "Dissociation as a Response to Extreme Trauma." In R. P. Kluft (Ed.), *Childhood Antecedents of Multiple Personality.* Washington, DC: American Psychiatric Press.

Rando, T. A. 1993. *Treatment of Complicated Mourning.* Chicago: Research Press.

Rao, M. R., R. A. Brenner, E. F. Schisterman, T. Vik, and J. L. Mills. 2004. "Long-Term Cognitive Development in Children with Prolonged Crying." *Archives of Disease in Childhood* 89:989–992.

Rauch, S. L., J. Metcalfe, and W. J. Jacobs. 1996. "A 'Hot-System/Cool-System' View of Memory Under Stress." *PTSD Research Quarterly* 7(2): 1–3.

Rauch, S. L., B. A. van der Kolk, N. M. Alpert, S. P. Orr, C. R. Savage, A. J. Fischman, et al. 1996. "A Symptom Provocation Study of Posttraumatic Stress Disorder Using Positron Emission Tomography and Script-Driven Imagery." *Archives of General Psychiatry* 53(5): 380–387.

Rizzolatti G, Fabbri-Destro M, Cattaneo L. 2009. "Mirror Neurons and Their Clinical Relevance." *Nat Clin Pract Neurol* 5 (1): 24–34. doi: 10.1038/ncp-neuro0990. PMId 19129788.

Rizzolatti, G, Sinigaglia, C. 2008. *Mirrors in the Brain. How We Share Our Actions and Emotions.* New York: Oxford University Press.

Ross, J. 2002. *The Mood Cure.* New York: Penguin.

Ruef, A. M., B. T. Litz, and W. E. Schlenger. 2000. "Hispanic Ethnicity and Risk for Combat-related Posttraumatic Stress Disorder." *Cultural Diversity and Ethnic Minority Psychology* 6(3): 235–251.

Sacks, S., J. Sacks, G. De Leon, A. I. Bernhardt, and G. L. Staines. 1997. "Modified Therapeutic Community for Mentally Ill Chemical 'Abusers': Background; Influences; Program Description; Preliminary Findings." *Substance Use and Misuse* 32(9): 1217–1259.

Saxe, G., B. A. van der Kolk, K. Hall, J. Schwartz, G. Chinman, M. D. Hall, G. Lieberg, and R. Berkowitz, R. 1993. "Dissociative Disorders in Psychiatric Inpatients." *American Journal of Psychiatry* 150(7): 1037–1042.

Saxe, G. N., Chinman, R. Berkowitz, K. Hall, G. Lieberg, J. Schwartz, and B. A. van der Kolk. 1994. "Somatization in Patients with Dissociative Disorders." *American Journal of Psychiatry* 151: 1329–1335.

Scaer, R. C. 2005. *The Trauma Spectrum: Hidden Wounds and Human Resiliency.* New York: W. W. Norton.

———. 2007. *The Body Bears the Burden: Trauma, Dissociation, and Disease,* second edition. Oxford, UK: Routledge Books.

———. 2012. Retrieved from http://www.traumasoma.com.

Schaeffer, J. Unpublished work sent to author via electronic mail.

Schlenger, W. E., R. A. Kulka, J. A. Fairbank, J., R. L. Hough, B. K. Jordan, C. R. Marmar, et al. 1992. "The Prevalence of Post-traumatic Stress Disorder in the Vietnam Generation: A Multimethod, Multisource Assessment of Psychiatric Disorder." *Journal of Traumatic Stress* 5: 333–363.

Schnurr, P. P., C. A. Lunney, and A. Sengupta. 2004. "Risk Factors for the Development versus Maintenance of Posttraumatic Stress Disorder." *Journal of Traumatic Stress* 17: 85–95.

Schnurr, P. P., C. A. Lunney, A. Sengupta, and L. C. Waelde. 2003. "A Descriptive Analysis of PTSD Chronicity in Vietnam Veterans." *Journal of Traumatic Stress* 16: 545–553.

Schore, A. N. 1991. "Early Superego Development: The Emergence of Shame and Narcissistic Affect Regulation in the Practicing Period." *Psychoanalysis and Contemporary Thought* 14:187–250.

Alan Schore, (1994), Affect Regulation and the Origin of the Self: The Neurobiology of Emotional Development, Lawrence Erlbaum Associates; 1 edition

————. 1996. "The Experience-Dependent Maturation of a Regulatory System in the Orbital Prefrontal Cortex and the Origen of Developmental Psychopathology." *Development and Psychopathology* 8: 59–87.

Seligman, M. P. 1998. President's Address to the 1998 American Psychological Association's (APA) Annual Meeting. Published as part of the "APA 1998 Annual Report" in *American Psychologist* 54(8): 559–562.

Siegel, D. 2010. Mindsight: *The New Science of Personal Transformation.* New York: Bantam.

Simeon, D., O. Guralnik, M. Knuntelska, and J. Schmeidler. 2002. "Personality Factors Associated with Dissociation: Temperament, Defenses, and Cognitive Schemata." *American Journal of Psychiatry* 159(3): 489–491.

Singh, S., V. K. Somers, M. M. Clark, K. Vickers, D. D. Hensrud, Y. Kornfeld, and F. Lopez-Jimenz. 2010. "Physician Diagnosis of Overweight Status Predicts Attempted and Successful Weight Loss in Patients with Cardiovascular Disease and Central Obesity." Am Heart J. 160(5): 934–42.

Society for the Advancement of Sexual Health (SASH). 2012. "Sexual Addiction." Retrieved from http://www.sash.net/en/articles/sexual-addiction.html.

Smith, Ann W. 1988. *Grandchildren of Alcoholics: Another Generation of Codependency.* Deerfield Beach, FL: Health Communications.

Spencer, S. J., and A. Tilbrook. 2011. "The Glucocorticoid Contribution to Obesity." *Stress* 14(3): 33–46.

Spiegel, B. R., and C. H. Fewell. 2004. "12-Step Programs as a Treatment Modality." In S. Straussner (Ed.), *Clinical Work with Substance-Abusing Clients,* second edition. New York: Guilford Press.

Stern, Daniel, 2010. *The Present Moment in Psychotherapy and Everyday Life (Norton Series on Interpersonal Neurobiology).* New York: W. Norton & Company

Stifter, C. A., and T. L. Spinrad. 2002. "The Effect of Excessive Crying on the Development of Emotion Regulation." *Infancy* 3(2): 133–152.

Stoddard, F., D. Norman, and M. Murphy. 1989b. "A Diagnosis Outcome

Study of Children and Adolescents with Severe Burns." *Journal of Trauma* 29: 471–477.

Teicher, M. H., S. L. Andersen, A. Polcari, C. M. Anderson, C. P. Navalta, and D. M. Kim. 2003. "The Neurobiological Consequences of Early Stress and Childhood Maltreatment." *Neuroscience Biobehavior Review* 27(1–2): 33–44.

Terr, L, 1988. "What Happens to Early Memories of Trauma?" *Journal of the American Academy of Child and Adolescent Psychiatry* 1: 96–104.

Thompson, Damien. 2012. *The Fix: How Addiction is Invading Our Lives and Taking Over Your World*. New York: Collins.

Ungar, M., M. Brown, L. Liebenberg, R. Othman, W. M. Kwong, M. Armstrong, and J. Gilgun. 2007. "Unique Pathways to Resilience Across Cultures." *Adolescence* 42(166): 287–310.

Uram, S. Lecture on Trauma. The Meadows, Wickenburg, AZ, July 19, 2011.

van der Kolk, B. A. 1987. *Psychological Trauma*. Washington, DC: American Psychiatric Press.

———-1994. "The Body Keeps the Score: Memory and the Evolving Psychobiology of Post-Traumatic Stress." *Harvard Review of Psychiatry* 1(5): 253–265.

———-2003. "Posttraumatic Stress Disorder and the Nature of Trauma." Pages 168–195 in M. F. Solomon and D. J. Siegel (Eds.), *Healing Trauma: Attachment, Mind, Body, and Brain*. New York: W. W. Norton.

van der Kolk, B. A., and R. E. Fisler. 1996. "A Symptom Provocation Study of Posttraumatic Stress Disorder Using Positron Emission Tomography and Script Driven Imagery." *Archives of General Psychiatry* 53: 380–387.

van der Kolk, B. A., and J. Saporta. 1991. "The Biological Mechanisms and Treatment of Intrusion and Numbing." *Anxiety Research* 4: 199–212.

van der Kolk, B. A., O. van der Hart, and J. Burbridge. 1995; 2010. "The Treatment of Post Traumatic Stress Disorder." Pages 421–443 in S. E. Hobfoil and M. W. de Vries (Eds.), *Extreme Stress and Communities: Impact and Intervention (NATO Advanced Science Series)*. Netherlands and Norwell, MA: Kluwer Academic Publishers; Springer. Also see Approaches to the Treatment of PTSD at http://www.trauma-pages.com/a/vanderk.php.

van der Kolk, B. A., A. McFarlane, and L. Weisauth (Eds.). 1996. *Traumatic*

Stress: The Effects of Overwhelming Experience on Mind, Body, and Society. New York: Guilford Press.

Vicennati V, F. Pasqui, C. Cavazza, U. Pagotto, and R. Pasquali. 2009. "Stress-Related Development of Obesity and Cortisol in Women." *Obesity* 17(9): 1678–83.

Watkins, M. 2012. "Thy Food Shall Be Thy Medicine." Retrieved from http://www.recoveryview.com/2012/03/thy-food-shall-be-thy-medicine/.

Wegscheider-Cruse, S. 1980. *Another Chance: Hope and Health for the Alcoholic Family.* Deerfield Beach, FL: Health Communications.

Weiss, D. S., C. R. Marmar, W. E. Schlenger, J. A. Fairbank, B. K. Jordan, R. L. Hough, et al. 1992. "The Prevalence of Lifetime and Partial Post-traumatic Stress Disorder in Vietnam Theater Veterans." *Journal of Traumatic Stress* 5: 365–376.

Werner, E. E. 1992. "The Children of Kauai: Resiliency and Recovery in Adolescence and Adulthood." *Journal of Adolescent Health* 13: 262–268.

Werner, E. E. 1996. "How Children Become Resilient: Observations and Cautions." *Resiliency in Action* 1(1): 18–28.

Werner, E. E., and R. S. Smith. 1992. *Overcoming the Odds: High-Risk Children from Birth to Adulthood.* Ithaca, NY: Cornell University Press.

———. 2001. *Journeys from Childhood to Midlife: Risk, Resilience, and Recovery.* Ithaca, NY: Cornell University Press.

Woititz, J. G. 1983. *Adult Children of Alcoholics.* Deerfield Beach, FL: Health Communications.

Wolin, S. J., and S. Wolin. 1993. *The Resilient Self: How Survivors of Troubled Families Rise Above Adversity.* New York: Villard Books.

Wolin S., and S. J. Wolin. 1995. "Morality in COAs: Revisiting the Syndrome of Over-Responsibility." In S. Abbott (Ed.), *Children of Alcoholics: Selected Readings.* Rockville, MD: NACoA.

Wolke, D., P. Rizzo, and S. Woods. 2002. "Persistent Infant Crying and Hyperactivity Problems in Middle Childhood." *Pediatrics* 109: 1054–1060.

Yalom, I. D. 1980. *Existential Psychotherapy.* New York: Basic Books.

Yates, T. M., B. Egeland, and L. A. Sroufe. 2003. "Rethinking Resilience: A Developmental Process Perspective." Pages 234–256 in S. S. Luthar (Ed.), *Resilience and Vulnerability: Adaptation in the Context of Childhood Adversities.* New York: Cambridge University Press.

Index

About the Author

Tian Dayton, MA, PhD, TEP has a master's degree in educational psychology and a Ph.D. in clinical psychology and is a board-certified trainer in psychodrama. She is also a licensed Creative Arts Therapist and a certified Montessori teacher. Dr. Dayton is the director of the New York Psychodrama Training Institute and was on the faculty of New York University's Drama Therapy Program for eight years.

Dr. Dayton is a fellow of the American Society of Group Psychotherapy and Psychodrama (ASGPP), winner of their Kipper Scholar's Award. She is the editor in chief of the Journal of Psychodrama, Sociometry & Group Psychotherapy, and sits on the professional standards committee for ASGPP. She has been awarded the Mona Mansell Award and the Ackerman/Black Award for contributions to the field of addiction and serves on the advisory board of The National Association for Children of Alcoholics (NACoA).

Tian created a model for treating trauma called *Relationship Trauma Repair, An Experiential Multisensory Process for Healing PTSD,* which includes a Therapist Guide, A Client Journal, DVDs, and guided imageries and is currently in use at treatment centers across the United States.

She is a *Huffington Post* blogger and has been a guest expert on NBC, CNN, MSNBC, CBS, *The Montel Williams Show, The Ricki*

Lake Show, The John Walsh Show, and *Geraldo* and radio. Dr. Dayton is the author of fifteen books including *Emotional Sobriety, Trauma and Addiction, Heartwounds, The Living Stage*, and *Forgiving and Moving On*. Her work has been featured in *The Process*, an award-winning docudrama that uses psychodrama to tell stories of addicts and ACOAs *Healing Childhood Abuse through Psychodrama*. For more information, please visit www.tiandayton.com and Dr. Dayton's blog on emotionexplorer.com

Dr. Dayton is the creator of the Internet's first interactive, self-help site, emotionexplorer.com.

Other books by Tian Dayton, PhD
Emotional Sobriety
Forgiving and Moving On
Trauma and Addiction
Heartwounds
The Living Stage
RTR Relationship Trauma Repair
Daily Affirmation for Parents
The Soul's Companion
The Magic of Forgiveness
Journey Through Womanhood
The Drama Within
Drama Games
Modern Mothering
It's My Life!
The Quiet Voice of Soul